PUPPET MASTER OR PAWN?

Raising successful, happy, and resilient children with needs, failures, self-discipline, and consciousness in a toxic world

Jesús Amaya, Ph.D.
Evelyn Prado, Ph.D.

Eloquent Books
New York, New York

Eloquent Books
An imprint of AEG Publishing Group
845 Third Avenue, 6th Floor—6016
New York, NY 10022
http://www.eloquentbooks.com

ISBN: 978-1-60860-790-7

Book Design: Bruce Salender

Printed in the United States of America

CONTENTS

Jiminy Cricket asks, "And what job will you have?"

Pinocchio responds, "Eating, drinking, sleeping, having fun, and living the life of a vagabond from morning until night."

(Carlo Collodi, *Pinocchio*, Chapter IV. Nuevo Talento Editorial)

INTRODUCTION

For the last five years, we have frequently traveled throughout Mexico, up to three times per week. This has become as normal to us as driving our cars to work every morning. Each time we are about to land, the captain and flight attendants inform us of the importance of not turning our cell phones on until we reach the terminal, but upon landing many passengers immediately not only turn their cell phones on but begin making calls. Even while the airplane is refueling, many passengers simply ignore all instructions. We have even asked some of them, "Why do you turn your cell phones on and not wait until arriving at the terminal?" All of them have answered us: "And what is the problem?" On another occasion, a mom told us about her sixteen-year-old son (a freshman in high school) who had been having some problems passing a class, so she hired a teacher from her son's school to help him. Since her son had practice four times a week after school, the teacher had to stay at school and wait for two hours after classes in order to help him. During the second class, the teacher called the mom and informed her that her son had not attended the session. The boy's father, upon picking him up, demanded an explanation as to why he missed his session, to which his son replied, "I had an incredible time with my friends! We went bowling." After telling his son that the teacher had waited for two hours after school to help him and that he had demonstrated a serious lack of responsibility, his son answered with no regard, "And what is the problem?" We are facing a society where comprehension and the difference between good and bad no longer exist. We are living in a society with the absence of conscience and free will and with what is known as the Jiminy Cricket deficit.

More and more often, we hear complaints from parents and teachers about a new defiance and indifferent attitude in today's youth. Discipline has become a serious and complicated issue for many people. Kindergarten teachers complain that their students don't obey them, challenge them, and even verbally insult them; all of this while the students' parents defend and justify their actions. They present emotional, social, and adaptive problems for their age. They have little capacity for interacting with other children, they don't follow instructions, have a low tolerance for frustration, and a low capacity for delayed gratification. They demonstrate low impulse control and are more aggressive at school. A large number of kids, between the ages of three and five, can't learn because they have a short attention span of no more than five minutes, or because they can't socially function in school. Studies show that at the kindergarten level, 35 percent of the children have discipline problems and defiant attitudes. This child profile didn't exist thirty years ago when teachers defined the kindergarten child as restless but obedient, docile and easy to educate.

University teachers indicate a tremendous difficulty in controlling their students: they sleep in class, don't attend, or frequently show up late. They constantly leave class or simply don't turn in any work. As a consequence, failure and dropout rates have increased over the last five years. Even more surprising is the fact that university students and their parents pressure teachers into passing them with high grades even though they haven't accomplished even the minimum requirements.

Parents tirelessly express their desperation due to their inability to supervise and control their children. Kids arrive home whenever they want, and it is impossible to ask them where they are going or what are they going to do because they will immediately respond in an aggressive manner: "Here we go again," "Don't you trust me?" "Why aren't you like other parents who let their kids go out alone?" or "I'm old enough to do whatever I want!"

Hara Estroff Marano published an article titled "A Nation of Wimps" for *Psychology Today* in December 2004 confirming that we are cultivating a generation of young people who are more fragile due to the fact that we overprotect them and plan their lives. Marano focused on the point that we protect kids from failing and trauma and that we practically run their lives. It is necessary for children to sometimes feel bad.

Children learn through all experiences whether they be good or bad, and through failing, children grow stronger. Marano further explained how this overprotection can cause children to weaken and fall into addictions, failing, indifference, narcissism, violence, and depression.

> **Young people today have fun only if they spend money, listen to music at a high volume, and consume alcohol.**

The following questions then arise: What is happening with today's youth? Where are the parents? And what are we doing about this? A four-year-old boy called his teacher an "old witch" because she wouldn't give him another crayon after he had purposely broken the one he had. Preschool children don't respect their classmates' toys, they draw on their notebooks, and hit others because they won't share a cookie. Three eight-year-old boys broke a five-year-old's nose because he wouldn't share his Nintendo© Game Boy. A ten-year-old boy from the Mexican state of Puebla committed suicide because his parents wouldn't let him go to a party. A fourteen-year-old teenager beat his mom because she wouldn't give him money to buy beer. Five high school students left the school grounds during class time to get something to eat and the speeding driver caused an accident in which three of them died. Recent college graduates quit their jobs to take vacations. And more young people, older than thirty, still live with their parents, don't work, don't have a girlfriend or boyfriend, and depend on their parents for everything. Upon asking all of these children and young people what they have learned from their actions their responses were: "Why do you make such a big deal out of this?" "Or what's the big problem?" "Or noooo!?" We have a generation of young people with a lack of conscience. An ignorance or fear exists when the time comes to set limits, when the baby decides where and at what time he will sleep, where a five-year-old has the latest trendy cell phone, and when ten-year-olds talk back.

Why are our children growing up out of control? The answer is that their lives are full of second chances, negotiation, relaxed consequences for their actions, minimal supervision and virtually nonexistent limits, a lot of freedom and money, having everything they need, a lot of overprotection; in other words, a total absence of authority and discipline exists. Permissiveness has grown like a virus.

There is no time to be a parent.

Experience and studies indicate that in order to strengthen our children and for them to make better decisions in their lives, they need three things from their parents: 1) unconditional love, 2) clear and fair limits, and 3) conscious consequences for their actions. This makes the big difference.

None of the previous generations have had an easy time educating and instilling discipline in their children. But today's generation is faced with more difficulties.

- Four times as many divorces as in 1960
- Seven times more single mothers than in 1970
- At least two television sets in every home

- 50 percent of Internet use in the ten to twenty year age
- Two and a half hours a day in front of the television
- Five hours a day in front of the television, computer, playing videogame, and using cell phones
- Nightclub and parties beginning at 11 at night
- Marriage, paternity, and maternity beginning later on in life (average thirty years old)

Do the delay in marriage and maternity make them better parents, busier parents, or more tired parents?

In reality, the modern family lifestyle has transformed dramatically during the last twenty-five years. We have kids saturated with extracurricular activities (soccer, taekwondo, ballet), internal family problems, and situations where children don't spend enough time with their parents to learn ethical and moral principles of acceptable conduct inside or outside the home.

Successful and happy children

Success and happiness are the two key elements for the parents of the perfect child. Happiness is defined as a mental state of harmony and completeness and success. Success such as a victory obtained in different areas and stages of life such as: academic, the arts, sports, and/or professional achievements. Unfortunately, parents are confused as to how to help the child achieve happiness and supply him with pleasures and freedoms trying to make him or her happy. They confuse success by allowing them easy victories, victories not achieved by their children's own merits. True happiness and personal success are gained only through hard work and personal sacrifice. The parents' purpose is to provide their children with the tools necessary to succeed.

The grave error that the present generation of parents has made is that they have forgotten to teach their children about self-control and self-discipline. Self-control is defined as the ability to control behavior, impulses, and to be constantly mindful. It is the capacity of controlling ourselves when necessary and recognizing something when it's needed even though we don't want to. The child who can't control his conduct when he is seven-years-old won't be able to control his temper and will have problems adapting and interacting with his peers when he turns eleven. Without self-control, serious problems of abuse and aggressiveness will be displayed towards classmates. In this book, we use the terms of self-control and self-discipline interchangeably.

Dr. Bernabé Tierno, philosopher and school counselor from Spain, states "... responsible parents have a clear understanding that loving a child is telling him what he doesn't like. Loving your children isn't giving them a false and temporary happiness by helping them avoid problems and difficulties but educating them to be independent, strong, and sure of themselves, with the ability to run their own lives."

We must avoid forming "Pinocchio children" and ruining their lives as a result of not being consistent and failing to instill limits. These children lack empathy, have a low tolerance for frustration, demand immediate privileges, and have virtually no control over their tempers. They have a challenging and manipulative attitude and only with great difficulty will they achieve maturity, independence, and happiness.

Gratification and permissiveness are two essential elements ensuring that our children won't suffer.

CHAPTER 1
GEPPETTO PARENTS AND PINOCCHIO CHILDREN WITH THE JIMINY CRICKET DEFICIT

Pinocchio's story begins

Carlos Lorenzini, the Italian writer better known as Carlos Collodi, introduced his character Pinocchio for the first time in *The Adventures of Pinocchio* in 1883. For almost all of us, the characters Geppetto, Jiminy Cricket, the fairy, and Pinocchio are well-known thanks to the popular Disney© movie that premiered in 1940.

The original story of *The Adventures of Pinocchio* doesn't represent a light fantasy or fun story such as the one presented in the Walt Disney movie. The original story shows the consequences of Geppetto's negligent and fearful attitude in Pinocchio's education.

In Collodi's story, Geppetto is a poor Italian carpenter and Pinocchio is alive from the very beginning of the story, even though Pinocchio was only a piece of wood that Geppetto would later transform into a mario-nette.

The Walt Disney movie (1943) leaves out a great number of details and which chapters were parts of in the original story, and changes that story in a dramatic way. In the film, Geppetto is a successful watch and toy maker. In the original story, Geppetto is a very poor carpenter. When the movie begins, Pinocchio is a life-less wooden doll that comes to life when the fairy grants Geppetto's wish of having a child. In the original book, Pinocchio is alive from the moment he is discov-ered in a piece of wood. When Geppetto begins to carve the wood to turn it into a puppet and finishes the head and mouth, Pinocchio laughs at Geppetto and sticks out his tongue. Once Geppetto has carved Pinocchio's arms, Pinocchio goes on to take off Geppetto's wig. Geppetto complains, "How do you dare disrespect he who gave you life? What I'm saying is that if you start out wrong, you have to correct yourself, if you don't want to go to jail." (Pinocchio of Carlo Collodi, Diana editorial, page 13). When he is finished with legs and feet, Pinocchio kicks him in the nose and escapes. When Geppetto finally catches up with Pinocchio, Pi-nocchio throws himself on the ground kicking and screaming. Poor Geppetto was accused of abusing Pi-nocchio and was thrown into jail. Pinocchio goes to Geppetto's house where he encounters Jiminy Cricket; Pinocchio goes on to hit Jiminy with a hammer, killing him. It is the ghost of Jiminy Cricket that appears in the rest of the story. Pinocchio demands to become the sole owner and heir to the house and refuses to go to school.

Collodi's Pinocchio is a doll that is not only naive but also impulsive, rude, selfish, violent, and incapable of controlling his own impetus. Pinocchio is a doll without morals due to the fact that he has no conscience and doesn't reflect on the consequences of his actions; the cricket becomes the voice of his conscience even though in the original story Pinocchio becomes angry with Jiminy Cricket and ends up squashing him. The cricket scolds Pinocchio for his pranks and mischievous ways and warns him about the dangers of laziness and cautions that if he doesn't go to school, when he grows up, he will become a perfect donkey. But Pinocchio doesn't listen and spends his time eating, drinking, sleeping, and living like a vagabond from early morning to late at night.

Once freed from jail, Geppetto meets up with Pinocchio and gives him his only food—three pears—and sells his only coat so that Pinocchio can have books and go to school. The next day on his way to class, Pinocchio sells his books for four cents and goes to see the puppet show. Geppetto makes the grave mistake of giving Pinocchio everything and asking for nothing at all in return. Later in the story, thieves tried to steal five gold coins from Pinocchio and choked him. A fairy rescued him and took him home.

Everyone was worried about his health except for Mr. Cricket who said that he was only faking and should be punished so that in the future he wouldn't really be choked. He opined that the best medicine for him would be a good swat on the behind. The cricket went on to say that Pinocchio didn't need doctors or medicine but instead a good stick; accordingly, Pinocchio is only a spoiled kid in need of a good spanking.

Pinocchio doesn't know the correct path to take and pursues a life of bad habits and laziness, surrounding himself with friends as dark and confused as he is. Regrettably, most people, like Pinocchio, follow the "easy path," ignoring the fact that another path, a "more complicated" but also "more rewarding" path, exists.

Ignoring all of the advice he received, Pinocchio decides to abandon school and go to Pleasure Island, a sort of child fantasy land, with his best friend Lampwick, to live free from all obligations, books, school, and spend all day playing. Lampwick would tell Pinocchio, "Listen to me. Come with us, and we will be happy forever." Even though, after only five months, just as Jiminy Cricket predicted, they all turned into donkeys. As a donkey, Pinocchio was sold to the owner of a circus to be tamed, where he was forced to endure hunger and hardship and was fed only straw and hay. When Pinocchio was crippled, he was sold to a fur trader who tried to drown him and take his donkey fur, but Pinocchio turned back into a doll. Upon escaping from the fur trader, Pinocchio is swallowed by a shark where he finds Geppetto. They escape through the shark's mouth and finally the fairy turns Pinocchio into a real boy.

Throughout almost the entire story, Geppetto is not involved in Pinocchio's education and upbringing. He was only involved at the beginning and at the end of his life. When Pinocchio's life couldn't become any more unbearable, he was swallowed by a giant shark. It wasn't until this point in time, when he was in the belly of the shark, that he could think about his life and then went on to make a radical change for the good in bettering his life and behavior. This wasn't until he had faced the consequences of his actions.

In the Walt Disney movie, the cricket appears as "Jiminy Cricket," and his advice is always ignored but he is never pummeled by Pinocchio. In the movie, Pinocchio represents a character who is simple and innocent, who doesn't know evil, and whose curiosity is the principal cause of his problems. On the other hand, Collodi's Pinocchio represents a character full of aggressive and rebellious impulses that are controlled only at the end of the story.

Pinocchio began his life as a rebellious child, inconsiderate and egocentric, who disobeyed rules and adults, always with dangerous outcomes. For example, instead of going to school, he sold his text books in order to buy a ticket for the marionette show. There he is imprisoned by the terrible marionette master and almost burned alive in the kitchen fire. In the Disney movie, Pinocchio's innocence and bad influences are what get him in trouble more so than selfishness and disobedience.

In the original story, we can see the kindness and sacrifice that Geppetto shows towards his son Pinocchio. In the first chapters of the book, there is a scene in which there is nothing to eat inside the house except for three pears. Geppetto offers them all to Pinocchio, who inconsiderately eats them all. (This scene, like others, was eliminated from the Disney movie.)

We know that Pinocchio was the creation of master carpenter Geppetto, who converted a piece of wood into a work of art. The work was undertaken with a love so deep that it was channeled, resulting in giving life to a doll made of wood, a boy made of good wood. Pinocchio had life, but nevertheless lacked a moral and ethical consciousness and wasn't able to differentiate right from wrong. Regrettably, most of today's children are just like Pinocchio. They lack a proper conscience and choose easy paths that can lead to their destruction without parental supervision and control.

Geppetto represents today's parents with his unconditional love for Pinocchio. He gave him everything he had without thinking of himself. He sold his only jacket to be able to send Pinocchio to school. Conversely, Pinocchio is disobedient and has behavioral problems, not caring that Geppetto would suffer because of him. Pinocchio grows up weak due the negative influences of his friends, like John Worthington Foulfellow, the fox, and Gideon, the cat. Because of Geppetto's inability to control his son, and because Pinocchio only cared about the easygoing life and having fun, Jiminy Cricket appears to advise Pinocchio on the good and bad aspects of life. Pinocchio represents today's children, children without adults who can guide and discipline them; those children with a lack of conscience (Jiminy Cricket) who will turn into a generation at risk due to the lack of strength of character to choose and act correctly. Jiminy Cricket appears on the scene to advise even when it is not to their liking or it is more difficult.

Geppetto's biggest mistakes

Geppetto's biggest mistakes include:

1. After creating Pinocchio, Geppetto was distant and absent from his life

2. Pinocchio grew up without parental supervision

3. Geppetto was scared to impose limits and have Pinocchio obey them

4. Geppetto gave Pinocchio too much freedom without responsibility and without allowing him to experience the consequences of his decisions. He didn't experience the consequences until the end of the story.

5. After Geppetto created Pinocchio, he allowed him to laugh and make fun of him. He couldn't make Pinocchio respect him.

6. The most important thing for Geppetto was making sure that Pinocchio was happy and avoided all types of punishment.

7. Geppetto gave Pinocchio too much and too soon without asking for anything in exchange.

8. From the beginning, Geppetto showed weakness in demonstrating authority over Pinocchio.

9. Geppetto spoiled Pinocchio by giving him everything he wanted even though he himself was left with nothing so that Pinocchio wouldn't suffer.

10. Geppetto overprotected Pinocchio so that he wouldn't have to deal with the consequences of his decisions.

11. Geppetto wasn't committed to guiding and disciplining Pinocchio's behavior, even when Jiminy Cricket was absent.

12. Geppetto was afraid to be strict with Pinocchio out of fear of losing his love.

Our children don't need Geppettos, they need real parents, present and firm. Children develop consciousness and strengthen it by constantly observing correct behaviors and their parents' morals, practicing these under their supervision on a daily basis. For this to be effective, parents need courage to be present, consistent, and firm to make sure moral standards are carried out or we risk having children without consciences.

Does my child suffer from Jiminy Cricket deficit?

Consciousness, in this book, is defined as the ability that human beings have to form personal judgments of a moral character over what is right and what is wrong. Consciousness is closely related to prudence. Aristotle defined it as the ability to comprehend the difference between right and wrong. Consciousness is considered an intellectual capacity that is learned through experience and which matures with age.

The knowledge or differentiation between right and wrong isn't enough to act correctly, it is also necessary to develop in children the will to act according to their conscience. The ability to differentiate between right and wrong isn't enough if the will isn't developed. Due to this fact, consciousness must also be related with strength. Greek philosophy defines strength as the courage to persevere in an action regardless of the types of temptation which may occur.

Within moral conscience there are certain categories:

- **Firm consciousness:** actions coincide with moral standards. There are no differences between actions and what is correct.
- **Lax consciousness:** consciousness which acts without moral rules. Everything is allowed.
- **Scrupulous consciousness:** Consciousness where everything is bad.
- **Cauterized consciousness:** no sensible consciousness. Such as with children who are exposed to violence, television, videogames, violence will seem normal to them and will cause them to act aggressively.

The Jiminy Cricket deficit shows up in two types of consciousnesses: relaxed and cauterized. A child suffering from Jiminy Cricket deficit will act without rules and values (lax consciousness). These are children with low moral and ethical sensitivity (cauterized consciousness) who live constantly exposed to a great number experiences with low moral values. A good conscience should act in the correct way, morally speaking, but even though our conscience tells us the difference between right and wrong we can act incorrectly. Prudence can tell us what should be, but it is strength that gives us the will to act according to conscience. Many kids know what is wrong, but group and peer pressure make them act against their own firm consciousness. Because of this, it is fundamental to develop firm consciousness (Prudence) and will (Strength) in our children so that they can lead their own lives and not be marionettes, like Pinocchio, controlled by their friends, fads, technology, money, and the pleasure of being accepted and having a well-known identity.

Living and facing consequences is one of the best ways a child can develop consciousness and act in the correct way. If a young man is responsible for an accident due to his driving under the influence of drugs and/or alcohol and his parents rescue him, he won't experience the consequences and think that driving impaired isn't wrong and will continue to do so. But on the other hand, if the young man pays the consequences, fines, jail time, and is not allowed to drive an automobile for a specified amount of time, he will not only realize that driving in this state is morally (as well as legally) wrong but also that it can also cause death to other people and himself.

Socialization is another way to develop a conscience. Interaction in society is fundamental so that children can develop their consciences. Unfortunately, children are currently more frequently growing up isolated from their parents and others. This is causing them to develop an "egocentrism," focusing all attention on themselves just like Pinocchio.

CHAPTER 2.
GEPPETTO PARENTS AND THE CONSEQUENCES

Adults today grew up in family environments where moral standards existed and strict rules were in place, rules which where accepted without discussion. Most of us grew up in environments with many requirements, where physical punishment was common. The father of the house was considered "the boss" of the family and applied the most severe consequences; the mother and children listened to him. Today, this is totally different. It is often the children who have the last say in the family; they constantly challenge and question anything the parents say or ask, "Why are you yelling at me?" when the parents speak to them in a firm voice. We are faced with arrogant and disobedient children.

Geppetto parents give in to any demand their children make. They consult, give a lot of explanations, and allow their children to make their own decisions without limits and without having to face the consequences.

The children are allowed to leave their houses without being asked where they are going or what they are going to do, much less with a set time to return.

> **They are splendid parents who give everything, but are absent when it comes to order, limits, and consequences.**

The parents of the past had tight supervision over their kids with clear rules and the consequences for breaking these rules, even though they lived in environments where few things could distract or hurt their kids. Television had only two or three channels, and the program schedule was well defined: in the morning and afternoon for kids and teenagers and at night for adults. We can still remember the old gangster show called "The Untouchables" that only adults could watch and being sent to our rooms so that our parents could watch it when we were young. There were few distractions in those days: playing, going out with our friends, sports, or television. Discipline wasn't as difficult because there were very few things to argue about and discuss. It was a simpler world with fewer distractions. Young people today have many more options, less firmness of character, and are more disobedience. As a consequence, they are in greater danger due to the fact that parents evade establishing limits, and that children are a lot more independent. Thirty years ago, parents were the ones who set the rules and children obeyed, not the other way around, which is what happens today.

Our children are living the Geppetto effect: an absence of rules and being provided with everything.

Even though parents spend more time with their children and give them everything, it appears that their children have become more insolent and aggressive. It seems that parents are scared of their own children, scared of them becoming angry or losing their love, scared of having them leave the house or commit suicide. One of the biggest family problems is the lack of authority over children. Parents don't want to make the same mistakes their parents made with them. We can't talk about an authority crisis but a lack of authority. Children and teenagers are growing up in environments where stability and the imposition of rules simply don't exist. We live in a century with the absence of authority in the home. It is important to tell our children "No!" We have to forget that they might be traumatized. It is necessary for our children to be a little traumatized. Extreme generosity from the parents doesn't promote gratitude or loyalty, but in fact makes children insatiable and ungrateful towards their parents. Tomorrow, these children will become immature adults incapable of facing challenges, incapable of lacking anything, incapable of failing, selfish, and solely motivated by their own well-being. This happened with Pinocchio; these are the attitudes he showed towards his father, Geppetto. The more Pinocchio received, the worse his behavior got due to the fact that he grew up with the Jiminy Cricket deficit, not having been able to develop his conscience.

Who are "Geppetto" parents? They are the parents who try to not repeat the mistakes their own parents made while trying to instill discipline. They try to make up for their absence from the home by giving in to every demand with few limits and no consequences for their children's actions. Guilt doesn't allow parents to act correctly towards their kids. Permissiveness doesn't allow their children to develop a Jiminy Cricket mind-set (their conscience), self-control, and form good work habits. They also create a capricious youth, with no motivation, without the capacity to overcome adversi-ties, and with a lack of respect towards their parents.

As we will see in the following chapters, it is neces-sary for our children to face frustrations and traumas so that they can develop a resilient attitude and the strength to face adverse situations during their lifetimes. What behavior characterizes a Geppetto parent? These are parents who set few limits: they overprotect and are very splendid. This causes disobedient, fragile, and immature children.

Permissiveness and the absence of Geppetto parents

The main characteristics of "Geppetto" parents are: weakness in discipline and indifference in the formation of their children's conscience and character. Permissive parents seek to please their children's every demand. They consult with them constantly, give them numerous explanations, and give them many liberties without taking into account their maturity level and their ability to assume responsibility for their behavior. The children are allowed to leave the house without being asked where they are going or what they are going to do, much less without having a specific time to be home. These parents are indifferent to the upbringing of their children and let others, such as school, grandparents, or other family members, do it for them. The parent-child relationship is reduced to a physical relationship lack-ing an emotional bond. Families eat together, but they are entertained by their videogames. There is a family dinner, but teenagers eat in front of the computer. Parents spend more than two hours a day driving their kids around while the kids are being entertained by a movie. There is almost no conversation. Families go on vacation, but the nanny takes care of the kids while the parents relax. In a small study, we found that 70 percent of mothers who left their babies (from six months old to two-and-a-half–years-old) in daycare for at least four hours a day, didn't work outside the home. When we asked them why they had left their children at daycare, the main reasons given were social events, rest, and exercise. Many schools successfully present the option of extended classes for children. Thus, children can stay in school from early morning until six or seven in the evening. Parents want only to feed, bathe, and put their children to bed. It is the parents' philosophy that the children will learn by themselves.

Then, Pinocchio stuck out his tongue.
Geppetto, to make life easier, pretended not to notice and went on with his work.
(Carlo Collodi, *Pinocchio*, Chapter III
Nuevo Talento Editorial)

CHAPTER 3.
GEPPETTO'S FIRST MISTAKE: TOO MUCH FREEDOM WITHOUT LIMITS AND CONSEQUENCES

Geppetto doesn't impose any limits on Pinocchio. In chapter three of the story of *The Adventures of Pinocchio*, the creation of Pinocchio from a piece of wood by Geppetto is vividly described. After finishing Pinocchio's face, he sticks his tongue out at Geppetto; after finishing his arms, he takes off Geppetto's wig; and after finishing his legs and feet, Pinocchio runs away. Geppetto never disciplined Pinocchio while all of this took place, he just went on working without applying any sort of corrective consequence.

Geppetto is a parent afraid of being strict and doesn't allow Pinocchio to live the natural consequences of his decisions. After finishing Pinocchio, the boy runs away and causes Geppetto's arrest. Upon arriving at Geppetto's house, Pinocchio falls asleep in front of the stove and burns his feet. The next day when Geppetto is freed, he makes Pinocchio a new pair of feet.

> # How many of us refrain from punishing our kids out of laziness or to avoid having problems with them?

Geppetto is characterized as being indulgent and permissive thereby causing problems of discipline and obedience. In our previous book, *Obedient Parents and Tyrant Children,* we described how today's parents belong to a generation of parents who obey their children's commands and not the other way around. Nowadays, parents ask their children for permission and apologize for any complications they might create. The hierarchy of the home has changed. In the past, when grandparents were invited to eat at the house, the mother would always serve them first and the children would be last. Today, the grandparents arrive for supper and the children are served first and the grandparents last. The hierarchy in the home must be recovered because we are producing children who are cruel and only care about themselves.

Children who are educated with permissiveness are not aware of what the real world means, and they don't learn about perseverance, sacrifice, and struggle to overcome difficulties. Permissive parents are character-ized by indulging their children with prizes and privi-leges without responsibility.

In a 2006 article written by Dr. David Bredehoft, "Influence of Childhood Overindulgence on Young Adult Dispositions," he identified young people who were educated in environments of indulgence and were perceived as having dysfunctional attitudes and were more fragile. He listed the characteristics of an indul-gent childhood as:

- Lack of obligations
- Too many toys
- Too much clothing
- A lot of freedom
- No consequences for breaking rules
- Too much attention and entertainment

In the past, strict parents were admired; today, they are seen as despots and tyrants. Nowadays, applying discipline is imperative, and it doesn't necessarily make one a tyrant. The word discipline is related to the word disciple which means "learns with others." **Discipline** *is the teaching of the rules of conduct with constructive methods that don't harm and are accepted through convincing and not by fear, with the result of having children develop self-control and character and giving them the ability to choose the correct options in their lives.* Obedience is peacefully accepting the will of oth-ers and discipline is carrying out what is needed through personal choice. Being strict isn't punishment; it is teaching how to follow through with commitment.

In the last few years, we have buried the limits be-tween adults and children. Small children decide where to sit, what and when to eat, five-year-olds have the latest trendy cell phone, ten-year-olds don't have a bed-time, and eighteen-year-olds have absolute freedom to come home at whatever time they like and in any state they choose.

Why are limits critical?

The United States is one of the few countries in the world that demands the minimum age to consume alcohol be twenty-one years of age. Other countries such as Japan and Iceland require twenty years of age to consume alcohol, South Korea requires nineteen years of age. Mexico, Chile, and Venezuela among others require eighteen years of age. While countries likes Spain, Germany, and Norway only require sixteen years of age. Why does this difference exist? Does it mean that the youth of Spain can control their alcohol consumption more than Americans? Does this mean that the youth of Germany is more mature than the young people of Iceland? The answer is no. The setting of limits must be determined according to the adequate use of liberty and responsibility. As children and teenagers prove better use of their liberty, the limits as a consequence tend to diminish or are altogether eliminated.

In the United States, a study was done during the late 1970s and the early 1980s to find a correlation between alcohol consumption and chronological age. This study concluded with the passing of a law in 1984 that prohibited people under twenty-one from consuming alcohol. And we quote: "All the evidence indicates that the increase in the legal drinking age drastically reduces the number of automobile accidents, suicides, and crimes with violence" (**Effects of Minimum Drinking Age Laws: Review and Analyses of the Literature from 1960 to 2000.** ALEXANDER C. WAGENAAR,

Ph.D., and TRACI L. TOOMEY, Ph.D. *Division of Epidemiology, School of Public Health, University of Minnesota).* The leading cause of death among teenagers throughout the world is alcohol- and speed-related automobile accidents. It is extremely important to review the minimum drinking age, and to also review the legal driving age. We must not be afraid to set limits! By doing so we can save many lives.

> **The children of today are governed by opinions and not by principles.**

One of the biggest mistakes parents today make is giving their children everything they want, and not simply what they need. In the following table, the column on the left contains some examples of what children demand while the column on the right contains what they really need.

What children want	What children need
Play, television, video-games	Reading
Money and permission	Responsibilities
Freedom	Consequences
Absence of a curfew	Limits and rules
Dinner in front of the computer	Family Dinner
Being the center of attention	Serving others
The right to drink alcohol	Teaching them to not drink alcohol
Receiving trust	Earning trust

Children out of control

Today's children are out of control; they threaten their parents with not loving them anymore. They yell, insult, eat in their homes just as if they were at a restaurant (with a menu), decide what, when, and where to eat, decide what time they will go to bed, and what TV shows they will watch.

The factor that has contributed to this is the change in the psychological theories that surfaced during the second half of the twentieth century telling us that tyranny and dictatorships had to be eliminated; where democracy must prevail in the family and that children must have the same rights as their parents. Children should participate in all family activities without exception, determining sleeping times, conversation, and which TV shows to watch.

> ## Our children are living in times of excess, without any restrictions, and they are convinced that nothing will happen to them.

.

One of these theories belongs to Dr. Benjamin Spock, an American pediatrician who died in 1998, whose book *The Common Sense Book of Baby and Child Care* was published in 1946 and translated into more than forty-five different languages. It destroyed the traditional concept of authority and discipline, taking on a more flexible and benevolent posture towards children.

Dr. Spock believed that when children misbehave, parents should engage their sense of responsibility and begin a discussion to persuade their children to change. It is important to talk with children and explain to them the reasons for the rules and obligations we have in place. After doing this once or twice, if the child doesn't want to understand or accept this, then our answer should be simple. "You do it because it's for your good and that's it," proffered in a kind but firm tone.

The need to "traumatize" them a little

There are many theories telling us that children are easily "traumatized" if we make them obey and punish them as a consequence of their actions. These theories bring about fearful behavior in parents and make them permissive. The fear of conflict, fear of losing their love, and blame make parents lenient and cause them to give in to all of their children's requests, never punishing them or teaching them to carry out their duties. Parents try to avoid the authoritarianism that they themselves lived through with their own parents and now try to gain their children's obedience through appeals and an infinite number of explanations and opportunities. Nevertheless, they always end up giving in to their children's demands.

Parents today are afraid of traumatizing their children. Nevertheless, one of the best consequences of telling your child "no" is giving him an adequate amount of frustration. An adequate dose of frustration helps form character and certain abilities to triumph in life. If these abilities are acquired from a young age, children will learn to tolerate and overcome obstacles without any difficulties and without their parents' help. One of the most important functions that parents must perform is developing their children's character so they can face obstacles in a world that is more complicated and dangerous. By making them face small frustrations, we will help them face their lives with independence and without fear of facing the consequences of their decisions. Their failures will help them develop resilience and perseverance.

Parents' main mission: make them happy and don't traumatize them.

It is perfectly normal for a child to want to be immediately pleased. He would rather have a soft drink than soup, or he would rather play before doing his homework. A child doesn't understand why he should wait. If it was up to him, he would do whatever pleased him all the time without restrictions. It is because of this that parents should intervene and make them understand there are more important things than eating candy or watching television. It is crucial to develop their self-control through discipline and the formation of habits. It is normal to find resistance and even aggressiveness, but we must not be afraid of their threats of not loving us anymore, or having them scream "I hate you" at us, or telling us that we're "very bad." Authority is essential in forming those habits that will control their behaviors in the future.

One of the biggest problems with teenagers today is the excess of commodities they possess: money, freedom, and fun. No persuasion or justification will convince a teenager that it is not correct to drink alcohol at this age and that it is even more improper to drink while driving. A teenager will understand this concept when he reaches adulthood, not before.

Supervision and open dialogue will help prevent, or at least postpone, addictions and delinquency problems. Every parent should be able to answer the following questions about their children: where are they, who are they with, and what are they doing right now? Parents must have the courage to prohibit things when they feel their kids might be danger: situations such as sleepovers or going on trips without adult supervision. This is not easy and even less so nowadays that independence is seen as something positive. We must be brave enough to tell our child "no" when he wants to watch "The Simpsons," or tell our ten-year-old child that we won't buy him "Grand Theft Auto IV©" or tell our fourteen-year-old daughter that she must turn off the computer and log off the Internet at midnight on school nights, or tell our seventeen-year-old son that he can't drink alcohol when he has a party at the house. All of this requires a lot of courage.

A mother was telling us how worried she was about the amount of alcohol consumed at teenage parties and said, "There are no chaperones or parents to watch over these parties!" We suggested that she not allow her thirteen-year-old son to attend any parties where there wouldn't be adult supervision. But she replied, "I have to give my son permission because 'all' of his friends are going, and by not letting him go, I would make him unhappy." We shouldn't complain that our children are exposed to great danger if we don't have the courage to tell them "no, not this time." Brave parents set rules and make sure they are obeyed; on the other hand, permissions are not consistent.

Consistency and not rigidness is the key to discipline.

When our children are young, democracy and freedom are limited. Order and structure are the firm basis to form a disciplined child. But once they reach adolescence, limits and consequences are implemented.

Few consequences will cause few responsibilities

If a girl forgets her doll in a restaurant, the mother runs back in to retrieve it. When a boy leaves his bicycle in the street and it gets stolen, the grandparents jump to the rescue and immediately buy him a new one. The main reasons that parents are negligent in applying consequences are ignorance, convenience, and fear. In our experience, we have observed that the majority of parents avoid implementing consequences for their children in hopes that their children won't be sad and become "traumatized," because if this happens they might go home and commit suicide. Parents are not aware that their permissiveness makes children more

40

fragile and puts them at greater risk to live with depression and think about suicide.

Children don't learn to be responsible because they don't face the natural consequences of their actions. To develop responsibility, children have to develop their capacity to make decisions and face the consequences themselves. Parents have to develop responsibility in the home from the time their children are young by giving them simple tasks like making the bed, taking care of the dog, or doing the dishes. According to studies, children who have obligations in their homes excel.

Consequences, when established, must be clear, fair, and consistent for them to be effective. If a teenager has a car accident as a result of driving under the influence, the natural consequence would be for him to not drive a car for a period of time. And we shouldn't feel sorry for him! How will he get to school or go out with his friends without a car? The answer is simple: have him take the bus. It is very important for him to live with the consequences of his actions. If a child fails a class because he didn't do the work, he should be grounded and not allowed to watch television, play on the computer or with his videogames for a month or until his teachers confirm he is turning his work in. Our son doesn't go out to play with his friends until his room is clean. We observe many parents who overly negotiate the consequences or give them three or more chances before punishing them, or who don't even punish them at all! We are raising fragile children.

Filled with rights but with few obligations

Rules for raising delinquent children

The popular juvenile judge from Granada, Emilio Calatayud, known for his wisdom in child education and guidance, published a book called *Reflections of a Juvenile Judge*. In this book he includes "Ten Steps for Raising a Delinquent." This book has the objective of raising awareness in parents of their responsibility in educating and raising their children.

Here we present the 10 steps:

1. Begin when he is young, giving your child everything he asks for: This way he will grow up convinced that the entire world belongs to him.

2. Don't give him any spiritual education: Wait until he is old enough and can decide for himself.

3. Laugh at his insults, stupid comments, screams, and challenging or impolite tones of voice: He will grow up disobedient, without authority, and disrespectful.

4. Never punish him and never tell him that something he does is wrong: Out of fear of "traumatizing" your child, he will grow up thinking he is a victim and blaming the world for everything.

5. Clean up every mess he makes, pick up his books, shoes, clothes, toys... Do everything for him; that way he will get used to passing his responsibilities on to other people.

6. Allow him to read everything that falls into his hands, make sure his plates and silverware are sterilized but that his mind is filled with trash (TV).

7. Argue and fight often with your husband/wife in front of your child: Troubled families will seem normal to him, and when the family breaks up for good, he will be neither surprised nor hurt.

8. Give him all the money he wishes to spend, this way he will grow up thinking that to have money you don't need to work, you just have to ask for it.

9. Satisfy all of his wishes, appetites, desires, and pleasures: Sacrifices and austerity could frustrate him.

10. Always agree with him and always take his side in any conflict he might have with his teachers, neighbors, etc.: He will invent any excuse possible not to learn and mature.

"Let's go home. When we get there, you will be punished."

To this threat, Pinocchio threw himself on the ground and refused to walk. The people began to stare at him and say, "Poor doll!"

(Carlo Collodi, *Pinocchio*, Chapter III.
Nuevo Talento Editorial)

CHAPTER 4.
GEPPETTO'S SECOND MISTAKE: OVERPROTECTIVENESS AND CHILDREN UNPROTECTED

In chapter seven of the *Adventures of Pinocchio*, Geppetto comes home after spending time in jail, and Pinocchio is very hungry because he couldn't eat in Geppetto's absence. Geppetto gives Pinocchio his only food-three pears-but Pinocchio couldn't peel them and threatened Geppetto that if he didn't peel them then he wouldn't eat. Geppetto then peeled the pears so that Pinocchio could eat.

Parents today don't allow their children to face situations of risk and failure and therefore don't allow them to face the negative consequences of their bad choices. The overprotective parent communicates and expresses his interest and affection towards his kids but doesn't allow them to live the negative consequences of any unwise choices they make. We parents perceive a dangerous and competitive world, and because of this, we justify our behavior when we overprotect our children. We prepare them for a complex world, but at the same time we don't allow them the opportunity to learn to make their own decisions and face the consequences. The world is rife with difficulties that children must learn to face by themselves without the protection of their parents, and we teach them that they are incapable of confronting this reality themselves. Here, we show some of the mistakes that overprotective parents make:

- Dress their kids so they won't be late for school, even when they can dress themselves
- Wake up their teenage son every morning for school
- Take his homework to school when he forgets it at home
- Give him his breakfast in the car on the way to school because he got up late due to watching TV until late the previous night
- Lie to the teacher by saying it was their fault that their son couldn't turn his homework in or that it was their fault that their son was late for school

He decided not to do his homework; we must allow him to face the consequences of his decision and accept any punishment the teacher might give him. This is the only way for him to become responsible. Parents tend to lie to avoid their children being punished. This occurs even at the college level. Last year, one of my students had me talk with her mother, who then told me her daughter had done her homework but had forgotten it on the kitchen table.

> **Efficient parents allow their children to make decisions, within certain limits, and have them accept the consequences.**

For the last thirty years, we have created many new laws that have given children many rights and have protected them. Children should be protected from any form of abuse and violence. But we have shifted to a dangerous area where we protect children from even the smallest failure. Frustration is a necessary experience that children need in order to learn to solve and overcome obstacles in the real world. The message we send to our kids is clear: "Poor thing, you can't do it; it's better if I do it or if I defend you." We don't trust them. We directly damage their self-esteem and make them feel useless and incapable of facing difficulties themselves. Parents don't want to see their children suffer, uncomfortable, or bored.

In our book titled *Tyrant Children Arrive at Work*, we have observed parents accompanying their teenage sons to job interviews and asking the interviewer to let them come in with their son because he is shy and won't be able to properly talk about how good he is. When will we let our children become truly reliant? Probably never. In this book, we describe how Boomer generation parents (born between 1950 and 1970), are the only generation in all of history to financially support their adult children instead of having their children support them.

Protected and supported

The other problem is that children consider simple or false justifications as real excuses, and we develop in them a feeling of "victimization." I am the "victim" and I am not responsible or at fault for anything, everyone else is. During adolescence and adulthood, maybe parents aren't around to protect them but the false justifications are always present. "I couldn't bring my homework, but it wasn't my fault because my mom forgot to buy ink for the printer" or "It's not my fault I'm late. My dad forgot to put gas in my car, and that's why I'm late." Super protection continues from the parents but now in a virtual way. The problem is serious in that children of all ages think that excuses and justifications are acceptable and exempt those from any possible negative consequences resulting from:

- "I didn't know..." Justification for not turning in homework because he wasn't present in the previous class.
- "My dad forgot to give me money for..." Justification for not bringing materials to class.
- "My mom wouldn't loan me her car..." Justification for being late to work.

"Bite them?" replied Geppetto. "I never would have thought, my son, that you were so delicate when it came to food. You must become used to eating everything."

Without another word, with a knife he peeled the three pears.

(Carlo Collodi, *Pinocchio*, Chapter VII. Nuevo Talento Editorial)

CHAPTER 5.
GEPPETTO'S THIRD MISTAKE: INFLATING A CHILD'S SELF-ESTEEM

Geppetto made Pinocchio feel that he was a special and unique doll from the moment he was created (chapter 3). From the beginning of the story, Pinocchio shows us how important he is and receives all the attention and privileges, more so than Jiminy Cricket, and even more than Geppetto himself. Pinocchio demonstrates domineering behavior like throwing Geppetto out of his own house even when he had lived in it for almost one hundred years. Geppetto committed the grave mistake of inflating Pinocchio's self-esteem so much that he felt superior to other people and felt that he had the right to abuse them.

Self-esteem is understood as personal judgment of your own personal value. It's the perception of superiority that one has of himself when faced with different life situations. An inflated sense of self-esteem, fictionally created by parents, develops the following behaviors: blaming others for self made mistakes (victim syndrome), apathy, aggressiveness, demanding of rewards for minimum work and effort.

Self-esteem is one of the most studied personality aspects of the last twenty years. It became popular during the 1990s as an answer to the repressive discipline that was exercised on children. It was developed as an antidote for unacceptable behaviors such as delinquency, depression, addictions, and academic failure. Parents thought that this would be the magic formula for children to have more self-esteem, make them strong enough to face social pressures, and solve their personal problems. Not only did the research find that a strong sense of self-esteem has little influence on preventing problems, on the contrary, a high sense of self-esteem, wrongly based, can cause serious aggression problems, social adaptation problems, narcissism (individualism), low frustration tolerance, and low expectations for personal achievement.

> ## Self-esteem is earned and not given.

A major concern exists today about giving children high self-esteem but forgetting to develop their character. More than producing happy children, we need to cultivate good and strong people.

Self-esteem is the good, bad, or mediocre perceptions one has of himself. I'm a good student, I'm bad at sports, or I'm mediocre at cooking. Generally, women have lower self-esteem than men. Self-esteem is gained through effort and personal achievement and not through merely participating. Parents have spent the better part of their lives raising their children's self-esteem. Society, parents, schools, and television have told us the importance of developing high self-esteem in children by using the following phrases: "You are unique," "You are very intelligent," "You are the best," or "You're a very special kid," whereby increasing their narcissism and centering all the attention only on them. We have heard many parents constantly call their kids "champion." "Very good, champion" or "You're the only person any good on your team, champion," and the funny thing is that he or she has never won a championship.

> **A child with a false sense of self-esteem won't have any goals and will become useless.**

According to American investigator, Roy Baumeister, high self-esteem doesn't help secure good grades or reduce violence. On the contrary, a high and false self-esteem will provoke an increase in aggressiveness and will also make children more deceitful. Children with false self-esteem present two dangers: 1) Not putting the effort into bettering themselves because they consider themselves perfect and liked by everyone, especially the weak, and 2) the fact they consider themselves superior to other people and justify any abuse. Australian investigator, Nicholas Elmer, confirms that self-esteem is related to attitudes of discrimination, abuse, humiliation, and driving automobiles at high rates of speed. It is also related to making people arrogant, comfortable, conceited, and boastful.

We must focus our attention on developing self-control and self-discipline in children. Self-control is the ability to preserve and continue and is considered a better indicator of success than self-esteem. With more self-discipline, children will finish their education and reduce the consumption of drugs, alcohol, and tobacco.

> **Yesterday, they had to fulfill their obligations; today, they demand that their rights be respected.**

Production of narcissistic children

According to Greek mythology, Narcissus was a beautiful young person who fell in love with his own reflection in a fountain. Without being able to take his eyes off himself, he jumped into the water and drowned. A narcissistic person is defined as someone who centers only on himself and lacks perspectives of other people towards him. He likes to be the center of attention and having all of his whims fulfilled. As mentioned in our book, *Today Tyrant, Tomorrow Cain*, narcissistic children tend to be more hostile and attack others, especially in school and within their families.

In his study, Harrison Gough affirms that the narcissistic phenomenon has grown during the last few years. Among teenagers, the feeling of importance towards themselves has grown from 12 percent in 1950 to 80 percent in 1980.

> ## Unlimited awards create a fragile and false ego.

Schools also actively participate in raising children's self-esteem in a false manner. Children who participate in athletic events obtain trophies and awards for merely participating. It doesn't matter how they place in competition, they obtain awards based on effort and not accomplishment. They are awarded trophies and medals even though they placed last in a soccer tournament. One of the biggest mistakes is acknowledging kids as winners when they don't deserve it. Competitive games are good for children in that they learn about frustration and failure as long as their parents allow it. On the other hand, when parents turn their kids into winners, without being deserving of it, kids learn that with little effort, and by merely participating, they will be rewarded and that success comes with little or no effort.

During the last few years, TV and other forms of communication have focused their efforts on creating a new generation of unique, special, and untouchable children, emphasizing the importance of developing a positive self-esteem. However, we have created a generation of young narcissistic monsters. "You're the best!" or "You're the only one!" Our children's generation is the first one where parents try to increase self-esteem without caring about the consequences. Most parents feed and increase their children's self-esteem in a false and incorrect way, celebrating the smallest and most insignificant accomplishments instead of celebrating true victories that take time and effort.

> ## Our son: Majestic from childhood to adulthood.

Many schools have eliminated awards for academic achievements such as conduct, punctuality, and attendance. School directors have told us they eliminated these awards because parents demanded that their children receive them, offering thousands of explanations and justifications and ending up removing their children from school because it was "traumatizing" for them. It is safe to say that today's generation has better self-esteem than previous generations have had. However, today's generation suffers from higher rates of depression. Children are growing up with more privileges very similar to those adults have, but children today are often shameless. They want to reach their goals aided at all times by their parents. By these actions, we are definitely ruining our children's lives.

> ## We turn them into adults too soon by giving them too much liberty and too many privileges without responsibility and supervision.

December 7, 2003, *Time* magazine published an article titled "Does Kindergarten Need Cops?" It described criminal behavior in children between three and five years of age. It mentioned that in 93 percent of the thirty-nine kindergarten schools referenced that today there are "more emotional and conduct problems" than there were five years ago. On August 15, 2004, the *Fort Worth Star-Telegram* published an article titled "Young Students Seen as Increasingly Hostile." This article mentioned that "kindergarten kids haven't learned to control themselves and are out-of-control. Students are more violent, lack discipline, and show little respect for authority." We can go on and on mentioning articles that show us how we are losing control and authority over our children (*Newsweek* issue 1) "How to say 'no' to your kids," published September 13, 2004 and issue 2 "Discipline: When kids attack" published April 5, 2008.

As time goes by, parents are losing more and more control over their children. Adolescence used to be the most difficult stage parents faced, but today a crisis exists in educating children when they are barely three–years-old. Three-year-olds have become defiant indi-viduals, demanding, and even aggressive. At the end of one of our conferences, a woman came up to us crying and telling us that she had a daughter who would hit and insult her and refuse to obey. We asked her how old her daughter was and she replied, "Only two and a half." While working with parents, we have observed a lack of competence that some can have in dealing with their children. Parents, especially mothers, show con-siderable anxiety and stress when dealing with their young children by themselves. They ask, "What am I going to do with my kid all day by myself?" whenever the child has a day off from school. We have observed kindergarten kids who grow up with inadequate adult role models and the absence of authority.

To be able to develop true self-esteem, we need to take the following elements into consideration:

1. Unconditional love
2. Firm and clear standards
3. Freedom with limits and consequences

Giving our children a false sense of elevated self-esteem is dangerous because it makes them feel superior and all-powerful, justifying their violence and aggression. A large number of bullies (children who abuse and humiliate their classmates) consider themselves superior and take advantage of their weaker classmates. They have almost no tolerance for people who are different from themselves and refuse to accept the fact that others deserve respect.

Giving them too much power is dangerous.

To reward or not to reward?

It is important to reward significant personal achievements. Parents today have become accustomed to rewarding their children for merely participating or to praise certain qualities. When our son gets an A in math we tell him, "Well done, you are a very intelligent boy." If he scores a goal for his team, we yell, "Great goal, you are the star player on your team." This is the natural response for congratulating them on their accomplishments because we feel proud of them and want to reinforce this conduct so that they are motivated to continue. We reward them time and time again so they can keep trying. But do these rewards motivate them to keep trying and make them feel good? On one hand, children like to be praised for their successes. On the other, too much praise can have a negative effect. Instead of making them feel good, we can cause more stress. If we tell them "You are very smart! I'm proud that you got an A on your test," they begin to worry about what we expect from them. Such as what would happen if they get a B? Will parents still think he is smart? And worst of all, when we have high expectations that aren't fulfilled, we tend to justify everything: Is the teacher unfair? Is the coach inept because he took my son out of the game and put him on the bench?

Trophies are no longer reserved for the best player or team. Now they are given out to everybody for merely participating in a tournament. The self-esteem of today is being fostered from an early age with praise and applause for every new step taken or small word uttered. Stars, ribbons, cheers, and hearty applause are given for small efforts and not for significant accomplishments.

Over praised generation

Over saturating praises and awards promote three attitudes: 1) Provokes more fear of not filling parents' expectations. Sooner or later, out of fear of not coming through for their parents, children will evade situations in which they can fail; 2) Children, when praised for their qualities, will no longer be motivated to perfect these qualities; and 3) A false sense of control will be created, and when he becomes aware of his limitations, his self-esteem will be negatively impacted.

We must focus our attention on effort and sacrifice as causes of success and not merely on the results. Instead of saying: "How smart you are!," we should say: "Because you did all your homework and studied, you were able to get an A in math. We are proud of you." Instead of saying: "You are a natural at scoring goals and you are the star on your team," we should say: "Since you have been practicing frequently, you have become a better soccer player and have scored more goals because of this. Congratulations." Children who receive too many rewards without deserving them become less motivated, show off more, and disregard others.

Children should be rewarded when they demonstrate good conduct and have significant results. Parents must not succumb to anger and their children's demands. Children should learn to control their emotions and frustrations.

> **Children who learn to deal with difficult situations and to delay gratification, grow stronger than those who don't.**

Bipolar parents in children's education

Bipolarism is a disorder characterized by extreme mood and personality swings. The two principal mood types experienced are depression and euphoria. Both of these are manifested in an unstable effect: one minute there can be extreme sadness, followed by almost immediately without reason extreme happiness. One of the main manifestations of being bipolar is experiencing opposite reactions in an extreme and exaggerated form.

> **Parents, on one hand, pressure their kids into being winners, and on the other, don't allow that to be demanded of them.**

Parents are worried and take great interest in making sure they protect their children from any negative incident that could harm them. But, children are allowed to watch TV, play videogames, go on the computer, and play with their friends all without any supervision. Parents take an extreme posture in overprotecting their children on certain occasions and at other times completely abandon them. Parents need to be informed about the real problems our children face, like alcohol abuse, pornography, and the Internet, so that measures can be taken to ensure our children's well-being.

Parents prevent at all costs their children from suffering any type of trauma, sacrifice, need, or sadness, but on the other hand, they pressure their children into being winners and successful people. How ironic! Joining these two concepts is impossible: becoming successful people without making any sacrifices or failures. Parents have to allow their children to face frustrating experiences that will help them develop their resilience. The word resilience comes from the Latin language, and it means to come back or return. This term is adopted by the social scientists and psychologists to define people who, even though they are born or live in situations of risk and failure, can work through these problems and succeed. In other words, the ability to overcome adversity and adapt to continue a productive life.

> # Parents who invent winners, make losers.

Parents demand the best from the schools that educate their kids, but at the same time don't tolerate homework, discipline, or punishment. Parents want kids to be responsible but don't want them to face the consequences when necessary. Studies show that children will never be responsible if they don't pay the consequences for their negligence.

For the last thirty years, schools have demanded greater participation from parents in their children's education, but few schools have taught parents **how**. Good parents are in constant contact with teachers and have requirements for their children.

My children first, then everything else...

Parents place their children above everything, even themselves. They want to prevent their children from occupying the second place in the family. When we were young and our grandparents would come eat at our house, Mom would serve our grandparents first, and then our father, and we would be the last to be served. Now, when grandparents come over to eat, Mom serves the children first, then dad, and the poor grandparents at the end. We have changed the hierarchy and the order of priorities in the family. These children perceive that they are on top, even higher than adults. This provokes more power and privileges for children and even humiliates their own parents.

During the last few years, formality and obedience towards adults has been condemned. Democratization and equality has been put in their place without consideration of age. Hierarchy has been destroyed, and we have entered the era of children addressing adults in informal terms.

Children call their parents by their first names. They also call their parents' friends by their first names. They call teachers and other employees by their first names, not even respecting school principals. All formality between children, young people, and adults has disappeared, and with this, the trust that children have in adults to educate, respect, and to be obeyed. This new order has created a generation of domineering and impulsive children who feel they deserve everything. This makes them less tolerant and justifies their aggressiveness towards others due to their feelings of superiority.

We put them before ourselves. We ask for their opinions in adult decisions such as: What school do you want to attend? Where do you want to go for vacations? What car do you want us to buy? We give our children the best things, and parents have to accept to the old or used models. For example, the parents give children the new cell phone and they keep the outdated one. The parents buy the child a new car and the mother keeps the old car. The parents buy them a new iPod© and the father keeps the old one.

With this form of hierarchy, it's difficult to get children to obey, because right now, adults serve children. Children and adults have the same rights, privileges, and freedoms: If Dad can do it, why can't I?

Pinocchio sold his books to buy a ticket for the marionette theater. And to think that Geppetto had to stay at home shivering from the cold, in a shirt with no sleeves, so that he could buy books for his son.

(Carlo Collodi, Pinocchio, Chapter IX.
Nuevo Talento Editorial)

CHAPTER 6.
GEPPETTO'S FOURTH MISTAKE: EXTREMELY PRESSURED AND CHILDREN WITH LITTLE DEMAND FROM THEM

It is common for parents to place enormous pressure on children. We want them to be champions when they are four, or have them become the best ballet dancer by the time they are seven. Parents justify having their children attend an early stimulation center so that children won't grow up "handicapped." These parents demand that their children master abilities such as reading and writing while they may not be mature enough, creating self-esteem and stability problems in the future.

We pressure them to be the best, and at the same time expose them early on in life to adult situations and contexts. We tend to try and make them grow up faster and have them face dangerous environments for which they don't have the age or maturity to face effectively. Last year, we were invited to a birthday party for girls between the ages of four and six. Instead of encountering *The Little Mermaid* or princesses, the theme of the party featured a soap opera. The young girls sang the soap opera theme song, dressed like the actors (who are teenagers), and danced provocatively, revealing their midsections just as in the soap opera. What are girls that young doing interacting with the soap opera theme? Now, a trend is beginning to emerge where girls between the ages of six and eight attend a spa. And instead of breaking a piñata or singing and dancing, they get their hair done, put on makeup, and get manicures and pedicures. Instead of receiving a bag of candy at the end of the party, they are given a bag full of cosmetics. Children's favorite TV show is The Simpsons. They demand cell phones from their parents and the newest MP3 players. They worry about dressing in style and having the newest technology in toys and cell phones. They compare themselves to schoolmates and friends and seek acceptance through sharing the same preferences, wearing tennis shoes with the Puma logo or a shirt with a crocodile on the left side.

In Dr. David Elkind's book *The Hurried Child*, he confirms that children today are pressured into achieving excellent performances, successes, and growing up as fast as possible. Producing more stress in children, more fears, higher emotional instability, loneliness, and more insecurities than their parents ever experienced in the past. Parents are trying to boost self-esteem in their children with all this pressure.

Teenagers are pressured into being accepted by their social group and responding to the social demands of their social context. Our children try to find their identity through material things like clothes with name brands, through vacations, or the cars they drive which gives them power and prestige in front of their friends. They are pressured into fulfilling their friends' consumption expectative, but are not expected by their parents to develop perseverance, effort, discipline, and responsibility.

Teenagers are pressured into creating an identity for themselves which is accepted by their friends, based on owning certain name brand objects that give them a certain status. Many parents, in hopes that their children won't be rejected, provide them with things, but not with the ideals of perseverance, responsibility, and work. We used to spend many hours practicing piano to perfect our playing skills, sacrificing TV, and playing with our friends. Today, parents pressure their children to be excellent piano players but demand few practice hours from them during the week so they won't feel pressured. We cannot have high expectations of them if we don't demand work and sacrifice. Besides, parents today can't bear to watch their children suffer, so they allow them to play games or watch TV instead of practicing.

If we want our son to become an excellent piano player, it requires effort, dedication, and discipline. Parents expect perfection without having their children suffer. If we want our children to read well, they need to practice reading, and the only way this can happen is by reading. In this life, children need to sacrifice small comforts, privileges, and freedoms to gain better qualities for the future. Parents want happiness for their children, but this can't be accomplished in the short-term. We need to give our children tools so they can succeed in the future. True happiness is constructed and accomplished through perspiration and ignoring immediate pleasure. What great happiness would come from accomplishing a goal that cost us effort and sacrifice!

Our children are pressured because they are experiencing situations they cannot handle due to the lack of emotional maturity and ability to handle them effectively. It is impressive how the criteria for censoring TV shows and movies have changed during the last forty years. It is amazing to see how movies that in the 1970s were classified for adults only, now can because during the daytime without any restrictions or censoring. Our children are exposed to a great number of different TV shows such as reality shows or soap operas where explicit situations are presented and our children don't have the maturity to comprehend or deal with them. Children are pressured into dressing and acting like teenagers when they are barely seven or eight-years-old.

Busy but bored

As time goes on, children and teenagers are exposed at earlier ages to adult situations and contexts. Children spend all afternoon in front of a TV screen, computer, or playing videogames thinking about the adult situations that they see or they participate in many organized after-activities such as Taekwondo, ballet, French, cooking, and poetry, so they won't be bored.

> **The important thing is to entertain them, make sure they're busy, and keep them away from danger.**

Parents use their children to dismiss their disillusions and frustrations from their own childhood, projecting onto their children what they couldn't be or do. Many think that by saturating them with activities they will be better prepared to face the competitive world where we live. Parents stimulate their children from the time they are in the womb with music by Mozart, or expose them from birth to intellectual stimulation videos and electronic games that teach reading and math. Unfortunately, there are no studies that indicate a relationship between early over-stimulation and intellectual development in the future. But negative side effects such as apathy, low self-esteem, and emotional instability can be developed. Some think that in order to be good parents they need to keep their children busy and entertained. This is why parents overload their children with activities and have their children watch TV, go on the computer, or play videogames in their free time to keep them busy and away from danger. And when the parents aren't around to entertain them, children complain, "Hey, Mom, I'm bored." And parents immediately intervene and look to entertain them before they become upset. Children need to confront their boredom and look for activities in which to focus their motivation and energy. Our parents never entertained us. When we had free time, we would spend it playing by ourselves or with friends.

According to the experts who study intelligence and emotion (Peter Salovey, Daniel Goleman, Howard

Gardner and Robert Sternberg), only 15 percent of personal and professional success is influenced by intelligence; the rest is influenced by emotions, social skills, and character.

Children with the game deficit

The Dutch anthropologist, Johan Huizinga, defines man as *homo ludus* (the playing man or man who plays). He defines the game as an art that involves imagination with its own rules. In his 1938 book *Homo Ludens*, Huizinga stated, "we need to play to become completely human." The game allows us to adapt to the world that surrounds us. Children today play more organized games than ever before. Children have more structured and organized experiences as do adults, and less free play, which is individual and creative. Free game stimulates and favors the development of self-control, inhibitive conducts, and attention. It helps social construction and prevents depression. It aids language and facilitates impulse control. The less free play children have, the more socially and emotionally incompetent they will be when they are adults.

The game is fundamental in developing self-discipline for children, where they define the rules themselves before and during the game. The game also helps control impulsive conduct, develops symbolic thought, practices planning and the acceptance of social rules. In lieu of indiscipline, the game requires the placing of limits obedience and respect to play.

The game has roles and rules in which the child has to give up his wishes and whims in order to play. Through the game, children control their reactive conducts, accept rules, and strengthen their tolerance for frustration and failure.

Organized games also have the advantages of:
- Learning teamwork and cooperation
- Making friends
- Tolerating frustration and losing
- Learning fair play
- Developing empathy for those who make mistakes in scoring a goal or basket
- Organizing personal time to combine sports with schoolwork.

Parents should be careful not to interfere by pressuring their children to only be winners and should not become involved in arguments with referees and coaches by not respecting their decisions during games. Children must learn to confront and respect situations of failure with security. Unfortunately, many adults show protective behaviors by justifying adverse situations, and thus, weakening their children's egos.

Parents have lost the perspective of childhood development. They don't trust children's independent learning and pressure them by involving them in a lot of organized activities. We don't allow our children to become bored and develop their own creativity and independence. After one of our conferences, a parent told us that one afternoon after picking up his son from soccer practice he asked how the practice went. The son replied that the coach never showed up, and when the father asked what they did, his son answered, "We didn't do anything. We just talked because no one told us what to do."

"These three pears were going to be my breakfast, but I gladly give them to you." And Geppetto went hungry so that Pinocchio could eat.

(Carlo Collodi, *Pinnochio*, Chapter VII. Nuevo Talento Editorial)

CHAPTER 7.
GEPPETTO'S FIFTH MISTAKE: GIVING IN EXCESS IN ORDER TO BE LOVED

Geppetto gives Pinocchio too much and too soon, making him an egocentric and narcissistic person with the rights to inherit his house while he was in jail. Geppetto gives Pinocchio his only food-three pears-so that he can eat. Then he sells his only coat so that Pinocchio can go to school. Geppetto gave Pinocchio everything he had so that his son wouldn't suffer. The father wasn't concerned about his own hunger or suffering. His only son was the most important thing for Geppetto.

Our children, like Pinocchio, are part of a generation that, as time goes on, want more and more. And even when they receive what they want, many times they aren't satisfied. Children who have received too much have difficulty surviving periods of need in their lives. They are more vulnerable and fragile.

> **Parents confuse excessive gift-giving with love.**

As we mentioned in the previous chapter, our children are pressured into being accepted and into reflecting an identity that is accepted by others. They pressure their parents into buying clothes and toys that reflect the status that is demanded of them by their friends. They always seek to stand out, be the first and exclusive, and own "name" brands that scream exclusivity. Not dressing like others, or not owning what others have, represents a threat to children's ego and self-esteem.

Parents are big spenders when it comes to their kids. They buy them too many unnecessary and extravagant items creating young narcissistic monsters that can't control their desires to immediately obtain more.

Name brands have become very important among teenagers, because name brands represent the ability to integrate with others and to strengthen children's self-esteem. Name brands develop traits in children such as confidence and acceptance. Our children don't want to feel left out or be alone, and name brands give them support and help them connect with others.

> **Children are close to their parents for economic support, but distant from them for emotional support.**

Now more than ever, parents of today give materialism great importance, and children grow up in a consumer oriented society. Children live to be constantly gratified and can't tolerate even the smallest needs. Parents put a lot of effort into satisfying their children's never ending wants and demands. Children demand ten times more toys, clothes, candy, and freedom than what they truly need. Excesses are harmful. Parents confuse generosity with unconditional love. If I love my kids, they shouldn't need anything. Effectively they shouldn't need love, dialogue, or respect; all of these should be present at all times. But we confuse loving our children with giving in to all of their desires.

Parents who give too much and too soon make their children realize that: 1) to obtain all the material things they want, it doesn't take hard work, small efforts will be enough to obtain large rewards; 2) self-esteem is strengthened by having and not by being; 3) it also generates dependence and conformance.

> **We give them so much and demand so little.**

Children need limits and structure in their lives so that they may develop responsibility and the capacity of self-control. However, parents who spoil their children cause a lack of development in certain abilities such as perseverance, effort, and tolerance of failure, and tolerance towards others.

The three types of parents who spoil their children and give in excess are those who:

- Give a lot of material things: Parents supply their children with clothing and toys. These children live with few needs and immediately have whatever they want. Children don't ask just for material goods, but they ask that they be "name" brands. They use only Puma© brand shoes and Ed Hardy© or Burberry© T-shirts. Even more shocking, these parents give their teenagers brand new cars!

- Give too much attention: These parents saturate their children with organized activities and leave almost no free time for them. They always want their children to be busy playing a sport or taking a class, or at least interacting with a videogame or the computer.

Excessive control causes dependence and boredom.

- Provide almost no structure and few limits: Children with few obligations at home will grow up with few abilities to survive.

For the first time in history, couples with children manifest less happiness in their marriage than those who do not have children. Parents express impotence in educating and disciplining their kids. These parents express anxiety when they need to take responsibility for their children's upbringing. "I don't know what to do with my son! He yells, insults me, and tells me I am a bad parent, and he is barely three-years-old." Now more than ever, parents enter into conflict when it comes time to discipline their children.

Nowadays, it seems as though mothers are the bad parents and fathers are the good parents. Due to the lack of parental authority, on the part of the father, mothers have taken control of discipline in the home. This causes stress in mothers who are used to receiving only affection from their children and not hate. This causes more friction between parents which exacerbates family problems. The excessive investment in children, as far as emotion, time, and money goes, destroys marital unions and causes an increase in divorces.

> ## We give them too much, too soon.

Parents who give too much and ask for too little

Parents flood their children with a lot of material goods, time, pleasant experiences, and little responsibility. They give too much, too soon, and for a long time. Giving our children too much prevents them from developing certain abilities such as perseverance, giving something up today to obtain better results afterwards, adequately facing obstacles and failures in life, and responding effectively to compromise. The risk in raising opulent children who have everything they want is that they won't develop the capacity to differentiate between a need and a whim. They will always seek to be understood by others, will never be capable of assuming responsibility for their actions, and will have few mechanisms to deal with boredom. We give them too much which causes problems in school, in their jobs, and in their relationships with others. We need to develop the capacity in children to limit themselves and face this world of consumption with moderation. A child who always receives and satisfies each of his whims will not have the composure to say no to addictions or sexual pressure when he reaches adolescence and adulthood.

Giving children too much relates to:

- Few obligations in household chores
- Too many clothes, toys, and attention
- Lack of limits
- No consequences for failure to obey rules
- A lot of entertainment for children

A fragile child seeks acceptance and formation of identity through fashion, money, and a car.

Extreme generosity in parents does not elicit gratitude in children. It converts them into unsociable, demanding people with the objective of spending however much they have and in the future becoming materialistic people with a low capacity for effort and work and incapable of handling situations of need. We are raising people accustomed to a certain social and economic level that they may obtain after thirty years of hard work or may never reach. We cause children from a young age to become accustomed to a luxurious lifestyle that took their parents many years of hard work to reach. One of the consequences is that children grow up feeling that they deserve this socio-economic level and wait for parents to give it to them. This creates adults who will still be dependent on their parents in the future, with low aspirations and living at their parents' expense. To obtain a better understanding of the consequences of giving to your children in excess, we recommend reading one of our books titled: *"Tyrant Children Arrive at Work: Professionals, occupied, connected, prepared, but still protected adolescents who deserve everything. How to understand them and what to do?"* published by Trillas and the article published by *USNEWS* on December 24, 2007 titled "The New Parent Trap: More boomers help adult kids out financially."

Our society is worried about creating children who receive immediate and abundant privileges, converting them into young people without aspirations, not willing to work or develop abilities and capacities that require time and effort. Our children will leave their piano lessons because acquiring certain abilities and seeing advances require time, sacrifice, and effort. They damage their self-esteem because they perceive themselves as incapable of learning how to play the piano and lose motivation in persevering and accomplishing bigger medium- and long-term goals. This is a generation that works only to obtain immediate and attractive rewards.

Delay in gratification

Delay in gratification is the ability to delay any type of privilege or immediate reward with the goal of obtaining a bigger reward in a longer period of time. Peter Salovey and Daniel Goleman, in their emotional intelligence theory, confirm that gratification delay is important in developing healthy, strong, and intelligent personalities. In our book, *Firm Parents for Dangerous Times: Raising successful children with difficulties and failures*, we establish the importance of having children experience small needs in order to develop the following:

- **Illusions and wish**: A child who receives and has everything no longer needs anything and loses the illusion of owning. One of the most important motivations in life is the wish to be someone or have something. Having too much, too soon, causes apathy and lack of motivation for work and sacrifice in our children.

- **Effort and work**: A child who receives everything and gives nothing in return will learn that in life working isn't necessary.

- **Caring for things**: The child who receives everything easily and immediately doesn't value his possessions and damages what he owns.

- **Indifference towards saving**: The child who receives everything immediately becomes accustomed to having all he wants and can't handle small needs to enjoy something bigger in the future and immediately wastes what he receives.

Every child needs to experience some cold and hunger so that he may value what it costs to be comfortable.

When Geppetto finished the feet, he felt a strong kick to his nose.

(Carlo Collodi, *Pinocchio*, Chapter III.
Nuevo Talento Editorial)

CHAPTER 8.
GEPPETTO'S SIXTH MISTAKE: LACK OF AUTHORITY AND OBEDIENCE

Geppetto never had authority over Pinocchio, not even while he created him. Pinocchio stuck his tongue out and laughed at Geppetto. And when he was finished, Pinocchio laughed at Geppetto, took off his wig, and ran away from home. Geppetto never had the strength to discipline Pinocchio and teach him to respect his authority and obey him.

Adults today grew up in family environments where firm rules were in place, were obeyed, and were accepted. Our childhood was surrounded by an authoritative environment where the father had the last say and the mother administered the home, closely supervising her children. Today, children have the last say; they defy and question adult instructions. We are facing an arrogant and disobedient generation.

Fear to traumatize

The democratization phenomenon has affected all social institutions, especially families. Almost all parents learned how to obey and give in to authority, but today's children don't obey, they question decisions, ignore orders, and demand explanations.

> **Now, adults adapt to the children, and these children don't learn how to give in.**

During the last few years, theories have emerged that affirm that obedience and firm discipline of children traumatize them. This has caused more permissive conduct. The fear of conflict and of losing their children's love threaten parents and force them to give in to all of their children's whims before disciplining them and teaching them their duties. "I'm the only one who doesn't go out!" or "All of my friends are going to the party!" These are some of the things children say to blackmail their parents and make them feel guilty. Parents feel guilty that their children might be rejected and their friends might make fun of them if they aren't allowed to go.

> ## Today's children aren't more difficult than previous generations; it's just that they face a more complicated world with fewer resources available to them.

Parents still feel resentment towards their own childhoods and don't wish to repeat the same degree of authority that they lived, though, when they were young. They seek obedience through begging and explanations and end up giving in to their children's whims. As a result, children end up doing whatever they want and then parents yell at them because they feel incompetent to orient their children.

A family environment with discipline favors the development of habits of self-control in children to regulate and delay gratifying their desires and increases their willpower. The existence of external controls facilitates acquiring internal controls.

Self-discipline is essential for academic success because it helps children acquire the following abilities:
- Following instructions
- Paying attention to instructions
- Controlling their temper with classmates and teachers
- Adequate social interaction
- Appropriate reaction to aggression
- Adequate use of free time

During the last few years, analyses have been made to determine the most prevalent causes for low academic achievement and failure in academic subjects. Among these causes are unprepared teachers, inadequate text books, and overcrowded classrooms. There is another fundamental reason why children have trouble and fail in school. It is because they lack self-discipline. We believe that many children have problems when it comes time to make decisions that require sacrificing immediate pleasure in order to gain rewards in the long-term. Children have conflict deciding to study before playing or watching television. Most children who can't control their conduct feel victimized and feel that everybody else is guilty. These children are also vulnerable to peer pressure and are more likely to drive at high speeds, consume alcohol, and use tobacco.

Some characteristics of children who lack self-discipline are:

- Constantly interrupting
- Refusal to obey
- Frequent tantrums
- Blaming others for their mistakes
- Aggression
- Defying adults
- Obscene language

Self-discipline is the ability to stop, think, generate strategies, consider alternatives, and more importantly, to analyze the effects of actions taken. A child with self-discipline internalizes rules and respects them even though there are no adults present. The child reflects before acting. Self-discipline is vital when resisting group pressure and delaying gratification to earn greater gratifications in the future. Studies confirm that if a child in kindergarten is able to delay consuming a tasty snack, the child will have better opportunities for academic success and mental and moral health upon reaching adolescence.

Discipline strengthens our children

Discipline stems from the word of Latin origin *discere*, meaning learn, and comes from the root *discipulus*, meaning disciple. One of the essential roles of parents is that of discipline, which helps their children learn. The goals of efficient discipline are to:

- Construct a healthy relationship with their parents
- Develop strategies for solving problems
- Secure a consistent and safe environment
- Produce desired behavior
- Develop self-discipline and control

Children with self-discipline and resilience persevere when it comes to difficult tasks, and even if they fail, their effort is constant. Self-discipline is the capacity to control impulses and direct actions towards fulfilling obligations, even though they are not enjoyable. Children with self-discipline can delay gratification and suppress their impulses until they can think of better alternatives and avoid the possible consequences of their actions.

We are a generation that give our children everything and ask for nothing in return. Children receive too much, too soon, and we demand very little. Children need to receive fewer material things and be given more:

- Persistence
- Delay of gratification
- Impulse control
- Tolerance of frustration
- Goal orientation
- Opportunity to acceptance of consequences
- Resilience

- Opportunity to observe and obey to rules
- Empathy
- Responsibility
- A sense of the meaning of life

Authors such as Yuich Shoda affirm that the ability to delay gratification is positively related to good intellectual and social performance. Shoda, in his article "Predicting Adolescent Cognitive and Self-regulatory Competencies from Preschool Delay Gratification," concluded that children who waited fifteen minutes for a reward had better academic averages, faced challenges more efficiently, and had a more effective personality during adolescence than children who could wait only a few minutes. And after thirty years, these children continued to have positive advantages.

> **Our children are growing up further away from us, more contaminated by TV and publicity, and with fewer tools to defend themselves.**

Children ruined by Geppetto's mistakes as a result of their parents' mistakes and inconsistencies in discipline are characterized as being excessively narcissistic and displaying immature conduct. Children with the Jiminy Cricket deficit lack empathy, demand countless privileges and permissions, demand their every desire be fulfilled, have great difficulty in tolerating frustrations and failures, and can't control their temper. Their conduct is defiant, manipulative, and even aggressive.

Parents need fortitude to deny privileges and apply limits for their children; courage to not allow their son to come into their bed even when he begs, courage to not take his homework to school even though it means he will be punished. Geppetto parents work hard to solve all of their children's problems and protect them from even the smallest frustration. They lie and justify their children's actions to other adults or to teachers when the children don't fulfill their duties. They make excuses for themselves for the orders they give, resulting in an image of inferiority, fear, and weakness.

Jiminy Cricket said, "Because you are a doll, and even worse, you have a head made of wood."

(Carlo Collodi, *Pinocchio*, Chapter IV. Nuevo Talento Editorial)

CHAPTER 9.
GEPPETTO'S SEVENTH MISTAKE: CREATING A MARIONETTE WITHOUT A CONSCIENCE IN A COMPLEX AND DANGEROUS WORLD

The biggest mistake Geppetto made was creating his son as a marionette who lacked a conscience and sending him off into a complex and dangerous world. What parents are capable of sending their children off into a perilous world without giving them the right tools to face it? Geppetto did this. He exposed his son who had no comprehension of good and bad and without having developed his will. He was unable to do good or to aspire to moderate himself when faced with dangerous wishes, to stop himself when faced with dubious situations, or learn to tolerate frustration.

Like Pinocchio, our children face threatening realities without their parents' support. They lack the ability to differentiate between good and bad, and they show weakness of character when they are required to act correctly, even though they don't want to, or to say no to a dangerous situation. Are our children prepared to face this world? Pinocchio wasn't prepared; he preferred fun to studying. He chose to kill his conscience (Jiminy Cricket) rather than listen to him, and he chose to sell his school books so that he could attend the marionette theater.

What is our children's attitude when it comes to the Internet, pornography, MySpace, videogames, alcohol, cell phones, nightclubs, and MTV? Do they have a developed conscience and enough willpower to face them? Our answer is no; our children are at greater risk than we were at their age. When we were young, few things could harm us. There were only three TV channels, parties began in the afternoon and were over by midnight. We drank only beer, and the worst type of pornography was a *Playboy* under the bed. Now we have to worry about situations that are more dangerous and critical: access to the Internet without any types of filter, cell phones, the abuse of beverages with high alcoholic contents like vodka or whisky and the mixing of these with energy drinks from an early age (eleven-years-old in boys and fourteen-years-old in girls), or attending parties that begin at midnight when most parents are asleep and can't supervise. We definitely live in more challenging times where opinions count more than principles, and this is combined with disciplinary absence of parents in the lives of their children, a lack of conscience, and a weakness of character to determine the correct paths in their lives. As a result, we have more problems related to depression, suicide, violence, apathy, medicated children, and low tolerance for frustration.

> ## Children with greater risks, without a clear conscience, without a strong will, and without parents

Many parents believe that giving their children complete freedom and placing trust in them will help them mature and prepare them to face challenges. For example, some parents tell us, "I teach my son to drink alcohol so he will know how to drink only with his friends." This is wrong! It is better to teach our children to say "no" to drinking. Giving children permission to drink alcohol without having developed their conscience and will favors alcohol addiction. Many parents respond, "My father gave me alcohol, and I'm not an alcoholic." We can't generalize what our parents did with us and subsequently do the same thing with our children. Times are much more complicated; children have more money, less supervision, no conscience, and little will. Be careful! We have raised children who are fragile and incapable of adequately facing the world.

To face this complex world, we need to regulate our children's freedoms and develop their comprehension between good and bad, and develop their character so that they may act according to their conscience.

A person without conscience and character is like a marionette, always exposed to the dangers of his surroundings and constantly in fear because he will move depending on which string is pulled (sex, drugs, or alcohol), without a conscience to guide and a will to turn away from evil. Children grow up without a will of their own and are at the mercy of their environment, just like marionettes that dance to whatever tune is played. They are pressured and think this is the way things should be: "All of my friends..." and "I'm the only one who..."

Our children drink more alcohol than we do, because this is the only way they can be accepted, and it can strengthen their identity in front of their friends. Children are more vulnerable to social pressures.

Parents today pressure their children so that they may be perfect, smart, handsome or beautiful, and faster than the rest. They only worry about their physical and intellectual perfection and forget to perfect their heart and soul. Making children kind, disciplined, and having strong character is also critical.

If we want our children to grow up without a conscience and with the Jiminy Cricket deficit, we should apply the following six rules:

1. Give them everything they ask for because they deserve it all
2. Make them feel they are superior to others and the world doesn't deserve them
3. Give them a lot, early on
4. Don't correct them out of fear of traumatizing them
5. Justify and defend their mistakes and misbehavior and always say they are correct
6. Never ask favors of them because it makes them sad. Everyone is at their service

Children without a conscience face destructive behavior

Educating and disciplining a teenager is painful and comparable to the work in childbirth; the only difference being that raising a teenager is a lot longer, between ten and fifteen years. More than ever, teenagers need emotional stability, their parents' presence, character, and discipline to face and overcome the destructive actions or environments that surround them.

Studies indicate that adolescence is the most critical period, because during this period, addictions to tobacco, alcohol, and/or drugs are more likely, as well sexual promiscuity and unplanned pregnancies are more common. Also a greater number of car accidents involving alcohol and speed occur, depression is more prevalent and suicides increase. To all of this we could add that maturity during adolescence is delayed and not reached until almost thirty years of age. In previous chapters, we mentioned the causes for the delay of maturity. Overprotection, giving in excess, not assuming consequences, and lack of firmness in setting limits are some of the reasons causing maturity to be delayed during this period. We must remember that our grandparents didn't experience through adolescence because they were married very young (average fifteen or sixteen years of age). Our grandmothers had their first child a year into their marriages, and our grandparents began working from the age of twelve or thirteen. They became adults and were bestowed responsibilities early on. Today, our children graduate from college and don't want to work because they want to get their master's degrees while parents pay for their extra studies. It was different for us. We finished college and worked for at least five years and then obtained our master's, but it was paid by us and not by our parents. Our children are not getting married until their late twenties and are having their first child after the age of thirty. We are lucky if our children get married at all because they want to obtain their advanced degrees, make money, travel, go out with friends, and after all this think about marriage. Meanwhile, we support them and overprotect them. Any money our children make is for them and none is for their parents. How times have changed! Before, we had to work to help out with our parents' finances. Now, we can't even retire because we have to continue to help our adult children financially.

> **Our children demand more, at an earlier age, and want more independence and privileges without restrictions or consequences.**

Our children are more unsupervised than ever when it comes to television, Internet, and videogames with more explicit themes with exposure and uncontrolled by parents and authorities. In August, 2008, we conducted a poll to determine what percentage of children and teenagers owned the videogame "Grand Theft Auto IV©," and we found that in ten elementary and middle schools polled, 70 percent of middle school students and 40 percent of elementary school students owned it. This is one of the most highly sold videogames and is in its sixth version. The first one was released in 2001. The classification level of the game is that of Adult exclusively due to obscene language, violence, and explicit sex. Studies show that children exposed to this material are more aggressive and show less tolerance and sensitivity towards others. Where are the parents?

Parents are distanced from their children, who are allowed to consume alcohol at parties with their friends when they are barely fifteen. We allow our daughters to bring their boyfriends home without adult supervision. We don't oversee the use of Internet. We don't know our children's friends and allow them to go on sleep-overs without adult supervision. A father told us that to see his son he needed to make an appointment because his son spent most of his time with his friends. Not too ago, the opposite occurred: friends were the ones who needed appointments and family get-togethers were common.

> **Internet and cell phones have increased cheap and superficial communication but have cheapened deep and significant communication.**

Many moms spend most of their afternoons taking their children to an infinite number of extracurricular activities. But instead of talking with their children, moms spend their time talking on their cell phones, and the children are entertained by a videogame or a DVD. At home, adolescents spend most of their time locked in their rooms while their parents watch TV, all resulting in little interaction.

Jiminy Cricket tells him, "The kids who rebel against their parents and abandon their home on a whim will never achieve anything in this world and will regret their decision sooner or later."

(Carlo Collodi, *Pinocchio*, Chapter IV. Nuevo Talento Editorial)

CHAPTER 10.
SELF-DISCIPLINE HABITS: AVOIDING GEPPETTO'S MISTAKES

Children have to learn that doing homework is more important than watching television, and that vegetables are better for you than chocolates. They need to regulate their whims in order to obtain rewards that are not immediate. This is called self-discipline. Children aren't born with this trait; it is taught, learned, and developed. This is one of the most important missions for parents: to form self-disciplined children.

The development of self-discipline and self-control are keys in developing a conscience in children. Self-discipline is defined as the internal mechanisms that strengthen will and character and act in a coherent way with thoughts and actions. It is the capacity of defeating all pressure that diverts a person from what is correct and true. It can also be defined as the capacity of doing what should be done, when it should be done, whether we like it or not.

We present the self-discipline habits that strengthen our character, and our Jiminy Cricket:

- Persistence
- Delay in gratification
- Impulse control
- Good behavior, even without the presence of an adult
- Effort and sacrifice in achievements and awards in the long-term
- Acceptance of the consequences of decisions
- Managing boredom
- Inhibition of distracters
- Beginning homework quickly
- Resilience
- Knowing and obeying limits
- Respect and gratitude towards others
- Living through failures and tolerating frustrations
- Having a sense of a true and real life
- Doing something because it is needed, even if it is not pleasant
- Parents and adults modeling the desired conduct for children

- Practice self-discipline habits over and over, even though they are not completely understood or fully embraced

Self-discipline is the best way to strengthen the will and conscience of our children. It is essential for them to be successful in their lives and upstages even intelligence. This capacity is more important to develop in boys than in girls. Parents and our experience show that boys are more fragile and have a greater Jiminy Cricket deficit than girls. Boys have a greater probability of academic failure due to increased apathy. They are bored easily, have low perseverance, inflated ego, goals that are too short-term, desire immediate gratification, have difficulty controlling impulses, low tolerance for failure, exert minimum effort, and have difficulty accomplishing tasks that are not fun and useful. Boys require more supervision and structure because their conscience and will are weak. It's fundamental for boys to succeed in school to develop their self-discipline. We must make them capable of doing their homework or of paying attention even though others are having fun and playing.

In a study published in *Psychology, A Quarterly Journal of Human Behavior* (Vol. 23, No. 1, 1986) titled **Self-Control and Achievement Motivation in Young and Old Subjects** by Dr. Robert F. McClure he asks, How is it possible that during the last years, students have raised their IQ (Intelligence Quotient) scores while their academic achievement test scores (SAT) have fallen? His answer: "Students have weakened their motivation for learning and have a lower capacity for self-control and self-discipline." We have very intelligent students who are unmotivated and have low willpower because their lives are controlled by opinions and not by principles.

> ## If there is nowhere to go, any road is fine.

Having a life project is essential in orientating and strengthening the conscience. Goals give the conscience a purpose. "In order to achieve my goals, what difference does it make if my conscience has a purpose or not?" In order to achieve an objective, many times it is necessary to sacrifice or leave immediate pleasures as to not stray from the road of the final objective. For this to happen, I need my child to have a clear and correct conscience and to develop the strength to have good self-control or self-discipline.

What is self-discipline?

According to a recent article by Angela L. Duckworth and Martin E.P. Seligman (2006) in Psychological Science, self-discipline is a better predictor of academic success than even IQ. "Most of the time, low grades among students are often blamed on poor teachers, boring textbooks, and large class sizes" the researchers establish. But we suggest another cause for students failing to exercise self-discipline . . . . We believe that many children have trouble making decisions that involve them to sacrifice short-term gratification for long-term gain. We can point to the power of self-discipline in sports, many athletes who triumphed over more talented players because they practiced more. We can define self-discipline as the ability to repress proponent responses with the objective of a higher goal. Examples of self-discipline include reading test instructions before answering the questions, watching TV after finishing homework, practicing piano lessons and then playing, taking notes in class rather than talking, paying attention to a teacher rather than being distracted, saving money in the bank rather than buying a toy, and persisting on long-term assignments despite tedium.

To develop self-discipline in children, it's necessary for parents to be role models and exhibit these traits. Children should see a clear relationship between what their parents say and do. Without this, children will lose credibility and their separation will be greater. Parents should make a habit of self-discipline every day of the year. If parents achieve the habit of self-discipline in their children then: 1) making correct decisions will be easier for them when faced with compromising and dangerous situations, 2) they will see acting correctly as something that is necessary and will achieve greater happiness, and 3) the sum of these habits will make the child more civilized and humane.

We present basic limits and rules for children:

1. Know where my children are, who they are with, and what they are doing.
2. Invite my children's friends to our home, to get to know them.
3. Eat breakfast, lunch, or dinner as a family at least five times a week.
4. Don't protect them from experiencing the consequences of their actions.
5. Supervise the content of the things they watch and games they play.
6. Avoid threatening punishments we can't carry out.
7. Children observe parents showing mutual love and respect.

8. Limit inappropriate information, especially from the Internet, videogames, and television.
9. Give them a sense of belonging in the family.
   a. Tell them about family roots and origins.
   b. Attend and participate in family events like parties, Christmas and related holidays, and New Year's celebrations.
   c. Demand they participate in household chores like picking up dirty clothes or washing dishes at least once a week.
   d. Make them participate in family events like dinner, attending church on Sundays, and going on vacations.

First habit: Controlling liberty with limits and consequences

Liberty is the capacity through which a person makes decisions without harming himself or others, and it is the ability to act according to one's own desire, all the while respecting the rules and norms defined by society. Freedom is a faculty to which we all have a right, but maturity and responsibility are required to accept the consequences of the use of freedom and also to respect the codes and limits of society.

Strategies to develop the habit:

1. **Don't protect children from the consequences of their bad decisions or negligence.** If the child forgets his homework at home, don't take it to school for him. Allow him to face the consequences of not going out to

recess to do it; or if the child leaves his bicycle in the street and it gets stolen, don't let his grandparents buy him another one.

2. **Supervise the rating of the content of things children watch or play.** If a child is less than ten-years-old, avoid permitting him to watch the Simpsons or soap operas. If the child is a teenager, avoid buying adult video games even though they may say, "All my friends watch it" or "I'm the only one in my class who doesn't have it." It's important for parents to supervise the elements (sex, violence, addictions) to which their children are exposed.

3. **Limit the use of Internet, television, cell phones, and videogames.** Obesity has become an alarming problem for children. Today's children spend almost four hours a day in front of a screen, reducing the time spent in games and physical activities. Children under five shouldn't spend more than an hour in front of a screen, and older children shouldn't spend more than two hours.

4. **Establish clear rules and fair consequences that can be carried out.** If your child leaves his toys on the floor, don't threaten that if he doesn't pick them up you'll throw them away. Avoid threats you won't carry out. Parents will lose credibility and children will grow up confident that they will never suffer the consequences of their negative conducts or actions.

5. **Establish a curfew for teenagers.** This is one of the most common problems parents face today. Teenagers demand liberty and independence but don't respect family rules. There should be a stricter curfew school nights than on weekends.

6. **Avoid second chances, especially if the cause was carelessness or forgetting.** Second chances are one of the worst poisons for creating a conscience be-

cause it doesn't allow children to suffer the consequences of their actions. The message is that anything can be done by children and is permitted.

7. **Privileges are earned and not given.** Watching television and going to the movies with friends are privileges that children must earn. If they don't finish their schoolwork during the week, permission for the weekend should be limited and any homework not done due to laziness should be finished on the weekend.

Second habit: Let them live the consequences of their decisions

This habit should complement the previous one. Experiencing the consequences of their actions is one of the most significant lessons that children must experience. Through consequences, children will learn to control and choose their actions. Unfortunately, parents protect their children from frustrations out of fear that they will become "traumatized." This produces immature people with low capacities for being responsible for their actions.

Here are some actions that will help develop responsibility in our children:

1. **Apply consequences to their decisions and mistakes.** If the child forgets his toy at the restaurant and he was warned not to take it, the consequence should be that the child loses the toy. Don't pity him. He must learn to be responsible for his belongings, and the child must not blame others for his mistakes. If you warn your five- year-old daughter not to throw her porcelain doll in the air because she will break it, and she doesn't listen and throws the doll and breaks it, she will have to do without the doll. And even though she cries and we feel sorry for her, she should have to make do

without the doll. Your daughter will learn to be more careful next time. And she will never forget the lesson.

2. **Life is hard sometimes, don't make it easy.** Parents protect their children from any uncomfortable or boring situation. We have noticed that when attending religious ceremonies how parents take up an entire bench and spread toys out all over the bench so their children will play and not be bored. These parents tell us: "poor them, if we don't bring their toys, they'll be bored." Or when we go to a restaurant, they bring along their Game Boy so the children will be distracted until the food comes. We need our children to be bored and have them develop the capacity to tolerate and endure these types of situations. What will happen when children are bored in school? And Mom isn't there to entertain them? They need to learn to self-regulate and be tolerant of difficult situations.

3. **Allow them to face failure situations.** Failure is another experience that, even though it is negative, it is fundamental that a child experiences it in his life. Parents protect their children from experiencing this, and thus children can't learn from it. If a child is the goalie on the soccer team, it is normal to see a mom or dad behind the goal coaching his or her son so that he will not be scored on or if the coach takes him out of the game and benches him, the parent will immediately disapprove of this or if a child cannot get first place at school, the parent will change the child's school, so that he may get first place. Our children need to be positively strengthened with their own personal goals and not their parents'. One of the most common mistakes parents make is always allowing his or her children to win. Playing bingo is a good alternative because winning or losing depends on luck and not mom and dad.

4. **Don't justify their failures**. Parents today protect their children from experiencing negative consequences in three forms:

a. Justify their children: Parents try to justify their child's bad performance in a game by saying, "My son didn't have breakfast and that's why..." or "My son had a bad night and because of that..."

b. Lying for their children: Parents lie to defend their children so they won't be punished: "My son did do his homework but I forgot to give it to him" or "I slept in. That's why my son was late to school."

c. Blames others: Parents project responsibility towards others. "Son, it wasn't your fault they scored a goal, the defense doesn't know how to play," or "It's not his fault he failed, the teacher doesn't know how to teach."

Children always receive justifications so that they won't have to be responsible for their actions. They develop victim-like attitudes: "It's not my fault, it's someone else's." Last semester, we talked with a student who was about to drop out of college because of his absences and tardiness. We interviewed him to determine the root of the problem, and he told us, "My absences and tardiness are not my fault. The college is at fault for having their parking lots so far away! I get to class five minutes before it starts because it takes me ten minutes to walk and get there." So then we asked him, "Why don't you leave your house earlier and get to class on time?" his answer was, "Why do I have to get up earlier to come? The school is at fault for not building a parking lot closer to campus." At the end of the semester, this student dropped out because he wasn't capable of adapting to this requirement, and we couldn't convince him that he was wrong because he felt as if he was the victim of the problem.

Third habit: Disinflation and making sure our children know their place

Modern psychology has emphasized for the last twenty years the importance of boosting self-esteem in children. This has been incorrectly interpreted, and instead of developing children's self-esteem as a result of their own accomplishments, parents try give it to them without asking for anything in return. We will offer advice to increase children's self-esteem in the correct and adequate way:

1. **Recognize only significant goals.** Many preschools have graduations for their students. Our question is: "From what are they graduating?" In this graduation ceremony, there's dinner, dance, cap and gown, gifts, and even a ring. When our children graduate from elementary school, graduation trips to foreign countries are organized and we ask ourselves the question: "From what are they graduating?" There is no question that these students have finished a stage in their academic careers and they deserve to be recognized. But a simple celebration is enough, not big and fancy one. Children learn that no matter how minimum or insignificant the achievement is, they will have a magnificent reward. We should wait until they graduate from college, and then we can congratulate them and celebrate.

2. **Applaud their effort not just their person.** Avoid saying: "You're the best." You must emphasize the process like: "Due to your dedication and efforts, you achieved first place." Applauding only their person creates conformance, apathy, and disregard for others due to a superiority complex.

3. **Fairness and equality are not the same things.** Parents and children have the same rights, but they are not equal. We observe a lot of children who interact with their parents as if they were friends; they defy, yell, and insult. Parents react timidly when it comes to their children's attitudes. We parents can make mistakes and children can let us know, but children must never disrespect you. There is a hierarchy.

4. **Learn to contribute.** Parents don't give children the opportunity to contribute in the house. That is, clean up their rooms or wash the dishes from supper. When children contribute positively in the house, their negative and antisocial conducts diminish. We must not be afraid to ask our children for favors, even though it means interrupting their favorite cartoons or their chatting on the computer. We must develop a service attitude in them, inside and outside the home.

5. **Privileges are earned.** Watching television, playing videogames, going to the movies are privileges that must be earned by carrying out chores and are not rights a child should have. Children's rights are clear: education, food, protection, etc. And all else are gifts that parents give their children because they love them and kids earn them. Don't give children anything they don't deserve.

Fourth habit: Less pressure and more demands

Our children are faced with more social pressures than we adults faced when we were young. Using certain name brand clothing, driving a sports car, drinking certain alcoholic beverages, and going to certain exclusive vacation spots are demands that our children make and we, as parents, give them. However, we ask them for nothing in return.

1. **Give them less of what they want and more of what they need.** We must give them less of what they demand like money, television, Internet, alcohol, cell phones, parties, and videogames, and give them more of what they need, like responsibilities, chores, homework, social service opportunities, consequences of their actions, and delay of gratification. Give them more time and attention than material items.

2. **More responsibilities in the house.** Children shouldn't have only one responsibility (performing well in school), they should form part of the family community and they should carry out their obligations such as bathing, walking the dog, cleaning the yard, picking up their dirty clothes, or watering the plants.

3. **Demand that they finish what they start.** It is important to develop persistence in your children even if they lapse into boredom or failure while they are doing their homework. This is fundamental in developing their strength, will, and character. They should learn to respect their obligations. If halfway through the soccer season our son decides that he doesn't want to keep playing because he is bored or for any other superficial reason, we should tell him he has a commitment that he must fulfill. And if, at the end of the season, he decides he doesn't want to play anymore, then that would be fine.

4. **Provide structure and a schedule**. Acquiring habits is a fundamental ability for survival, not only for school, but also for everyday life. In order to learn this, routine, discipline, and structure are required from a very early age. It is essential that children have a schedule for their activities and that it be respected, keeping in mind certain exceptions and including flexi-

bilities. During the week, this schedule should include at least the following activities, during periods of school and vacations: eating, personal study, school, sleep, recreation, chores, personal grooming, and family get-togethers. Respecting the schedule will lessen the pressure because they will need to spread their time and effort equally over a greater number of commitments and activities.

Fifth habit: Forming character by first satisfying with needs and later with gratification

Our children are part of a generation that lives surrounded by consumerism where materialism turns their wishes into reality. And if parents give in to all of their material desires, we will be basing their self-esteem on material goods and name brands rather than on their accomplishments resulting from long, sustained effort.

1. **Limit their privileges**. This can be accomplished by controlling the use of television, Internet, videogames, computer, and cell phones. Having an established schedule and limiting access is vital. For example: Watching television, playing videogames, or talking on the phone is not allowed during a family meal. Additionally, the child should be limited in television use, computer use, and videogames to no more than two hours per day.

2. **Delay in gratification**. Children need to learn how to wait and not satisfy their whims immediately. If your child wants ice cream, you can buy it for him, but tell him he can only eat it after supper. If the child doesn't accept the conditions and throws a tantrum, you tell him, "Now, not even after supper." Parents must be

the ones to establish authority and must establish conditions and not allow the children to do it.

3. **Don't give them everything "name" brand.** There is a pressure to excel through the ownerships of goods.

4. **Value savings.** Our grandparents knew that if they didn't save money during their youth, then they would have problems in old age because they would no longer be able to depend economically on their parents. They worked hard, had few luxuries, and saved money so that they could have a better future along with their children. Today, our children want to spend their money as soon as they get it, and they spend their parents' money even faster. We need to open up savings accounts for our children and teach them that when they receive money, only a part of it should be spent on personal necessities and the other part should be saved. If our children want something expensive, we should tell them, "I will pay for part of it, and you can save money to pay for the rest." This way, saving money will make sense to children.

Sixth habit: Going back to obedience and respect

Parents don't want to make the same mistakes their parents made: blind obedience, no dialogue, fear of authority, inflexibility, rigidness, and physical punishment. Many of us live in fear of a strict and authoritative figure. Parents today want to get along with their children and build relationships based not on fear, but on friendship and mutual trust. Unfortunately, we have lost the balance and are afraid of correcting our children or disciplining them because we think that we may lose their love (you can find more information on this topic in our book: *Obedient Parents and Tyrant Children: A generation that wants to be friends and forget about being parents).* Parents who are not respected and succumb to their children's demands will have trouble controlling and gaining their children's respect in the future. Following are some strategies parents can use to obtain their children's obedience.

1. **Don't tolerate obscenities**. Today, parents tolerate their children's obscenities: "Mom, shut up, you don't know. Stay out of it!" And even worse, parents apologize for their children's mistakes. Other adults sometimes find the spoiled kids' behavior amusing: "Leave him alone, he's only a child and he looks cute." We should immediately stop them right there even though we are in a public place. We have frequently observed that children sometimes hit their parents, and the parents ignore and tolerate this behavior. There are no consequences from the parents towards this type of behavior.

2. **Demand "please" and "thank you."** Courtesy is the first step towards respect. Children and teenagers don't discover the importance of kindness and how this will help them succeed in life by themselves. We have to teach them. We must show them from when they are little the magic words such as: please, thank you, I'm sorry, excuse me, good morning, etc.

3. **Teach them to give in.** When we were young, we learned to obey and give in to our parents' demands, and even today we still give in, but now to our children's demands. It's important for our children to have some influence on decisions that may not be very important to the family, for example: places to eat dinner or what movie to see. Most of the time children choose and parents give in, but it is now necessary for parents to choose and for children to give in. It is normal for

children to complain, but we have to tell them, "Today we choose, and next time you choose."

4. **Respect hierarchy.** Children should learn that if they are seated and their grandmother arrives, they should be the first ones to stand and give up their chairs. Usually, the opposite happens; parents stand up instead of having their children rise. Parents don't want to bother their children because they might be offended. Children shouldn't be comfortable when adults have to be uncomfortable. If the child doesn't want to give up his seat, then he should be made do so.

5. **Be parents and not friends.** Children have only two parents and many friends. Parents should not be afraid of losing their children's love because they applied a fair consequence. No parent wants to see his or her child sad or hurt; it's the last thing we want. But a child is like a tree, it needs to be trimmed so it can grow strong and not grow bent.

Seventh habit: Become emotionally close to them

Our children are granted freedoms, privileges, and money, but they lack the significant parental presence. Even though parents spend time with their children, they are isolated. It is as if they were living among strangers. They all live under the same roof, but large walls separate them. Children are happy as long as parents ignore all rules and negative consequences, and give their children as much money and freedom as they want. And parents will be happy if their children aren't an obstacle in their social lives. Today, children and adults live more distanced from each other and money is the only thing they have that brings them together.

1. **Parents must display togetherness.** If we want to build better relationships with our children, children must first observe this type of relationship in their parents. If children observe fights and arguing, instead of respect and trust between their parents, it will be difficult to build a solid relationship with them. Parents should be the living example of what a relationship is supposed to be like.

2. **Create and respect family rituals.** Eating dinner as a family and visiting grandparents are rituals that create a sense of belonging among family members. Just because your children are teenagers shouldn't justify their being excused from these rituals. We can be flexible and allow them to miss certain family events, like a birthday party, but they cannot miss significant events like Christmas and comparable holidays or New Year's celebrations. It is important for children to accompany parents on vacation, to religious ceremonies, or visiting relatives on Sundays to create a relationship with other family members.

3. **Eating lunch or dinner together as a family at least five times per week.** Studies show that families who eat together reduce and prevent problems of addictions, delinquency, and the occurrence of premature sex in children and also form better family relationships.

Eighth Habit: Creating children who aren't marionettes: with character and Jiminy Cricket

As mentioned in chapter 6, our children are pressured because they face a world that is more complicated and demanding, containing such distractions as pornography, MySpace, Facebook, videogames, nightclubs, and sports cars. They face this world without adequate tools such as conscience and willpower to succeed. Our children are marionettes like Pinocchio. Marionettes that are influenced and moved by their surroundings, without the character needed to succeed. In conclusion, we present some alternatives:

1.   **Develop a sense of true meaning in life.** Children should visualize clear goals so they can work towards achieving them. Children should broaden their vision for the long-term and discipline themselves so they can sacrifice and put the effort into achieving their goals.

2.   **Don't give children toys, money, and attention in excess.** Don't try to buy their love by satisfying all of their desires and demands. Don't give children a false sense of accomplishment by bestowing on them awards and prizes they don't deserve. They have to earn privileges with personal accomplishments in the long run; these accomplishments cannot be immediately given.

3.   **Create happy children who have goals, requirements, needs, and consequences.** We must prepare our children as well as possible, but we will never accomplish this by being permissive and by giving them everything. We must raise strong children (disciplined, with willpower and purpose in life) with Jiminy Cricket, who can successfully face pressures, needs, and failures in their lives.

LaVergne, TN USA
10 December 2009
166585LV00002B/1/P